The wind blew gently
through the trees and
across a lovely blue,
clear lake. Beyond the
lake stood Mt. Konocti
strong and silent, in
the midst of the milky
sky and the soft spring
sun shine. Clear Lake Oaks California, the year
May 1, 1942. There in a small house on a back
street, I was born. Born in the peace of the
landscape, only to begin a childhood of air raid
drills and a far away war.

My mother said, "When you were four months
old, I took you out in your buggy and left you
under a tree. When I came back and started to
bring you in the house, you started screaming
and kicking and grabbed a handful of my hair. I
never seen a kid that loved the outdoors so much.
Then when you were two and a half, you ran away
from home. I couldn't turn my back for a moment.
We found you at the drug store ordering a milk
shake."

When I was three years old we moved to the Mt.
Diablo mines about fifteen miles outside of Concord, California, in the mountains below Mt. Diablo. The Quicksilver mines stood crude and brown,
with rock piles heaped all around, roads of dirt
twisting up to the buildings and to the hills behind, that were being pulled down in the search
for ore. I remember the men busily working, leaving the upturned soil in towering piles. Working,
digging, sweating for the precious ore that was
held in the earth.

Below the mines were two rows of houses placed
neatly on two dirt roads. Eight houses, painted

white or brown at one time but the red dirt that rolled down from the mines left them a redish brown. The women could only wash on sundays, because of all the dirt. They all said, "Wouldn't it be nice to hang out a wash without worrying about all that dam dirt from the mines?" It seemed like my mom never had enough time, she was always so busy cooking, washing, scrubbing the floors, and nothing would stay clean. My dad would always say, "Don't you ever do anything. This place looks like a pig pen." Then he would spit on the floor.

My mother had this washing machine, with a ringer, I really liked that old washing machine. I loved to watch her run the clothes through the ringer, all the water being squeezed out of them, until they got all stiff and then she would try and put them in the basket to take outside but not very many of those stiff clothes would fit in the basket and then they were really heavey. When she carried them up the hill to the clothes line she could not drop any of them in the dirt or she would have to start washing them all over again.

When my mom washed my clothes, she would always pick them up with a stick and shake them before she put them in the washing machine. I used to put lizards in my pocket and forget to take them out. Mom said, I was awful, always playing with lizards and frogs and bugs. This one day she was washing, a sheet got caught in the ringer and I went to help her and got my fingers caught in the ringer. She really got mad and almost cryed. "Oh Sharon what am I going to do with you?"

It was a hard life living there at the mines, my father working long hours and my mom fighting the dust and the dirt and raising two small children and a teenage boy. My father and all the men that worked in the mines were men that believed in being tough and they liked to cuss, drink, and fight. From the time I can remember being alive, I can remember witnessing my father's fights. I was scared when all the yelling and cussing was

2

going on and when all the blood went everywhere
but when I saw my dad so happy about winning, and
when he said, "I can lick any man twice my size,"
I thought, "I'm sure proud of my dad." My mom did-
n't like fighting and said it was not right and
her and dad use to get in arguments about it but
dad just kept on fighting and drinking.

There was three acid ponds up the road from
where we lived. The water from the mine ran down
the hill and filled these ponds with water and
acid. People used to throw dead cats and dogs in
the ponds and we would watch them swell up and
then see how many days it took before the acid
would eat the flesh off the bones. We used to
skip rocks across the acid pond too.

One of the guys that worked with my dad had
poison oak very bad all over his hand. The guys
knew he was new and did not know very much about
the mines, so they thought it would be a real
good joke to tell him to put acid water on his
hand. "Yep Charlie, if you go and put some of
that good old acid water on your hand, that will
cure it right up."

Well, as usual I was around where I should
not have been. I went over to talk with Charlie
and his wife. She was taking the bandges off his
hand. It was about three days after he had put
the acid water on his hand. It was not a hand
she unrapped. It was a bloody, green blob, with
stuff running out of it. I felt this sick wet
feeling comming over me and sweat started pop-
ping out on my forehead and then I felt weak and
everything went black. I was on the floor face-
ing the wall I didn't know what happened, I guess
I fainted. I turned around and Charlie and his
wife were just standing there looking at me real
funny. I jumped up and ran out the door. I ran
and ran, my heart beating and the dizzy sweaty
feeling clutching at me. I could not run anymore.
I fell on the ground and tried to get my breath
back. Then I noticed the pretty white clouds in
the sky and the blue all around them and I smell-

3

ed the grass, and smokey licked my face. Smokey
knew something was wrong. He sure was a smart dog.
    Smokey and I spent most of the time playing in
my secret valley and away from the mines, where
the dirt and the digging could not reach, where
blue bells and poppies grew wild. The oak trees
and pine trees were filled with singing sparrows
and woodpeckers. I could sit by the stream that
flowed through the rocks and watch it move. The
water was clear and it was so pretty with green
grass around its edges. I could sit very still up
the hill from the stream and wait for the deer to
walk up to the creek and drink. I could catch a
bee in my hand and it would not sting me. I can
remember running through the grass and thinking
at any minute I would begin to fly. I can remember searching the tall oak trees for a limb to
make a sling shot. Sometimes I would go up by
the mines and climb the ore belts and hide in the
rock crusher and watch the rocks fall in the dump
trucks, after being crushed. Vic, the land lord,
did not like any kids around the mines and especially the rock crusher and he always tried to
catch me. There were holes up in the mines that
had no bottoms and I found this one and spent a
lot of time dropping rocks in it trying to hear
them hit the bottom but I never did hear any rock
make a sound after I dropped it in that hole.
    I had this duck named Zeekie, and he use to
follow me everywhere. Zeekie would look at me and
"Quack" he acted like he was really talking to me.
I used to go out and dig worms for him and mom
said if I didn't quit feeding him all those worms,
he would bust wide open from eating so much. Smokey and Zeekie were my best friends. I never knew
ducks could be smart, my mom said, "That duck's
almost human." Zeekie used to grab my sister's
dress and pull her around. I told all my friends
about how smart Zeekie was but they said I was
lying. So I went to get Zeekie. He was supposed
to be in the chicken pen. Well, Zeekie was gone,
and I looked and looked for him and I could not

4

find him anywhere. I decided to make an investigation and find the dirty rat that had stole my duck. My first clue was a feather pointing toward this big kid's house. That was it. I knew who did it, that big kid stole my duck. So that night I told my mom that I thought I knew who did it. She said, "You don't know who did it so just shut up and sit down and eat dinner." My brother Bob was sixteen and he was sitting at the table with my little sister Kerry and my dad, laughting like mad. "Come on, Sharon, why don't you have some of this good chicken."

My dad and my brother killed Zeekie and then they wanted me to eat him. I really hated them for that.

We had company and I brought my favorite lizard in to show everyone. My mom said, "Get that thing out of my house." My little sister said she wanted to hold my lizard, and my dad made me give it to her. She got scared and squeezed its guts out. My very favorate lizard too.

Vic, our landlord, was a real nice old guy, accept when he caught me playing in the mines. My dad and brother used to laugh and talk with him all the time. I used to stand and listen to them. My dad didn't think kids should talk much, so I had to be careful or he would slap me in the mouth. This one day Vic was talking about a job he had for someone that knew how to run a jackhammer. I said, "Vic, why don't you give me the job?" They all started laughing. "I bet I can run that jackhammer, and I need a job."

Vic said, "O.K. kid, you be at the scales at 8:00 tomorrow." The scales were where the dump trucks weighed there loads of rocks. My mom told me he was just saying that. No six year old could run a jackhammer, but I went anyway, and spent two hours waiting and Vic never showed up.

I found a big jar and thought, "Is my mom ever going to be happy when I show her this jar I found!" I was real careful carrying it home, but tripped over a rock and fell on it. I broke the

5

jar and I felt terrible because my mom would have really been thrilled with that jar. She could have used it for her canning. So instead of making mom happy I cut my old arm and got in trouble.

Then one day my mother told me I was going to first grade. She sat me down and curled my hair, and right then I knew I was not going to like school. We went into Concord fifteen miles away and my mother left me there. She said a bus would bring me home. The teacher told her not to worry about me. At recess these boys started calling me names and running and everyone was looking at me, so I picked up this rock and threw it at them. Well, I missed them and hit this girl in the foot. The teacher came over and shook and shook me and really scared me. I felt awful. I was sorry I hit that girl but I sure would not of felt bad if I would have hit those boys.

I was always fighting after that first day and I would come home with my dress torn and all messed up. My mother would really get mad. "I can't afford to buy you clothes and have you tear them up. Look at all the washing and ironing I have to do. Oh, Sharon, I had your hair looking so nice. Why can't you be good?"

The teachers did not know what to do with me and I spent most of my time in the office. My dad said, "If anyone says anything to you, slug them in the mouth." So I did. My mother told me to keep my mouth shut, and try and get along with the kids. I would get so mad at those kids and I always ended up in a fight.

Somewhere over the mountains there had been a big war and we had to be careful because someone might come over and blow us up. So we practiced air raid drills. It seemed like we sure spent a lot of time on the floor under our desks.

I would sit in class and look out the window at the birds and wish I could fly away. I hated school and it just kept getting worse. The teacher would say, "Sharon, you're a disgrace the way you act. Sharon, quit looking out the window. You

come up here and count to ten, on the board. You're
the only one in class that can not count to ten."
All the kids started laughing. I wished I was in
my valley and a big bird would come in and peck
that teacher on the nose.

My brother got the belt and said he was going
to beat me if I did not count to a hundred. I could
not count to ten. He hit me and yelled at me until
I learned to count to a hundred. I never seen so
many numbers in my life, I didn't think I could
ever count to no hundred. Then the old teacher never ask me to count to ten again. After I went and
learned to count to a hundred. They just ask me
something when I don't know what the answer is.
My dad said he should ought to give me a good beating for causing so much trouble.

Smokey walked me to the bus stop every morning
and he was there every night to meet me. My mom
said she did not know how he knew when I would
be home. I got eight F's on my report card but
the teacher said she had to pass me because I was
too big to stay back. The last day of school I
got to wear my overalls to school and I was really
having alot of fun cracking walnuts and eating
them. There was a big walnut tree right in the middle of the school yard. I could climb the trees
and not worry about my dress getting torn up. I
could play baseball with the boys and slide. I was
really having a good time when these girls started
laughing at me. "Look at that dirty tom boy. Wait
a minute. Is that a boy or a girl?"

I said, "Go to hell."

"Did you hear what she said? Let's go tell the
teacher."

The teacher came walking over to me all red
faced and mad and I was really scared. "Sharon! I
doubt if you will ever learn to act like a lady
and wearing those pants does not make you even
look like one, and I will not have any more of that
truck driver language around the rest of the children."

"Sharon talks like a truck driver! Sharon talks

7

like a truck driver!"

I spent the rest of the day in the office.

I really liked summers, we had some rocks out in front of the house and my brother Bob showed me how to catch lizards with a piece of grass. I played marbles with Bobby and Jerry, two neighbor boys. We also walked on stilts, and practiced shooting our bows and arrows, make sling shots, and played football and baseball.

I'll never forget the day my mom's best friend Velma found a case of her husband's wine under the house. She came up to our house and told mom and they decided to get my dad's twenty-two and line up the bottles on a dirt bank down by the garbage dump and target practice. They laughed all the way down the road, then they lined up the bottles of wine and shot them all. They really looked funny laughing and shooting those wine bottles.

My dad went and bought a fifth of wine and my mom grabbed it out of his hand and threw it against a tree. He got in the car and went down and bought a gallon. I wished I could go outside but it was dark. The only time I was happy was when I was outside.

Chapter Two

There, were five kids in
our family, but Jim, and
Billie my older brother
and sister, did not live
at home. Jim and his wife
lived in Stockton, Calif-
ornia and Billie and her
husband lived in Oakland,
California. My brother
Jim was a real hero to
me. I use to tell my friends about how he was in
the Navy and was sent to Japan. They said, I was
a lier and I didn't have no big brother. When
Jim came to visit he walked around with me so I
could show all the kids. Jim got this gun barrel
out of a house that had been burned down and
widdled a stock for it. He fixed up the gun as
good as new. It was a single shot twenty two. He
took me out target practicing, we shot at tar-
gets or beer cans. This one day we were walking
back to the house and he said, "Kid you see that
pine tree? Well see that sparrow, if you shoot
that sparrow, I'll give you this gun."
     I did not want to kill anything, but I wanted
that gun, I stood there looking at that bird.
     "Dam it shoot, give me the gun you probably
can't do it."
     I aimed the gun and shot, the bird fell out
of the tree and layed dead on the ground. My brother fead it to the cat, that old cat just grabbed that bird up and ran graweling, chewing on
it. I felt like a murder, and I thought about
what my mom said about how awful it was to kill
anything. I wanted that old gun and up and killed
for it, I sure was not a very good person. My brother said, "That kid just up and blew that dam
bird out of that tree, I really didn't think she

could shoot that good." Yea, I killed that bird
and I did not feel good even if Jim did.

My dad and two brothers got drunk, and there
was a big fight. My dad called Jim's wife a bunch
of names and said, "My son is young enough to be
her son." June got mad and said, she was never
comming back to that dirty hill and then she started crying, then they left. My mom and dad got in
a big fight and she said, "You and your drunks
and fights always wreck everything." My dad sat
there at the table drunk and his face was all red
and then his eyes got all watery and tears fell
on his cheeks. "None of you give a God dam about
me, you think your so God dam good, you slut."
My dad always cryed, but my mother never cryed.
My little sister was scared and I told her everything was alright. My dad went to bed and then
my brother Bob, gave me a shot of whiskey. It tasted awful and burnt my throat and it made me sick.
My brother said I was drunk, when I tryed to walk
and could not very well, he laughed and laughed.

My little sister gave chicken pox to my brother
Bob and me. The only place I had the chicken pox
was in my hair, no one had ever seen that before.
It was Easter vacation and Bob had to stay home
and could not go any place. He was so mad and sit
around cussing and I laughed and laughed and he
said if he did not feel so bad he would get up
and beat the shit out of me. I laughed and laughed.

Me and my little sister and two girls that were
visiting the neighbors went for a walk in the
hills. We were having a good time, the girls were
singing and pretending they were movie stars. They
laughed and made up big stories, one talking and
the other laughing and my little sister's eyes
were big and she was smileing. We picked blue bells,
and poppies and sung more songs. I was walking a-
head of them, I was showing them the way to my secret valley. Smoky was walking beside me and then
all of a sudden he started running ahead of me on
the path. The bushes rustled but I thought it was
just the wind and then something jumped and Smoky

10

cryed out in pain. It was a rattle snake. We all
got rocks and went after it and I smashed it's
head in. Smoky was laying by the path and his
whole back end was paralyzed. We took turns carrying Smoky and the snake and hurried as fast as
we could. We all knew he would die if we did not
get him to a vet. We got home and I found mom,
and she got one of the neighbors to take her and
Smoky to the vet. The snake we killed had nine
rattles. Everyone said they had not seen a snake
with nine rattles very often, around there. Most
of the rattle snakes around there had between one
and five rattles. My mom was really mad at me,
she said Smoky saved my life, if it would have
been me they could not of got me back in time.
She told me never to go back up there again. In
a couple of weeks Smoky came home and he was alright. I sure was glad to see him.

I was going to train Smoky to be a show dog.
I put a rope around his neck and tryed to lead
him around the yard. My dad seen me and got mad.
He put a rope around my neck and tied me to the
steps in front of our house. The rope hurt my
neck and I was scared when it started to get dark.
My mom screamed and yelled and finally he took
the rope off my neck and let me come in the house.
I never put a rope around Smokeys neck again and
I was sorry I did not know how awful it was to
have a rope around your neck.

This old man, Mr. Clayton and his wife, lived
up the hill and there daughter was in the Napa
state hospital. She escaped and was running through
the hills when they caught her. They had to take
her away in a straight jacket. The cops were driving up and down the hill and everyone was talking
about it.

"Isn't that awful that woman running around
here mad?"

"I sure can see why she is that way with a mother and father like she has."

"That old man running around killing everything that moves."

11

"Someone ought to do something."

"There hauling her away in a straight jacket."

Mr. Clayton, was always carrying a gun around killing something. I did not like him and I kept away from him. One day I saw him sitting on a tree stump entranced in one of his favorite hobbies; shooting birds and if they had not died, he would hold them in his hands, letting them peck at his flesh. By the time they were dead, his hands were dark red with blood. I felt sick, when I saw that and it was awful the way the birds beat against his hands and the awful crys they made.

Smoky disapeared, and we looked all over for him. This pup, specks, that my brother brought home was with Smoky and a day later she came back with her throat cut and bleading. We thought maybe a mountain lion or bob cat had attacked her and Smoky while they were out hunting. Smoky loved to go out in the hills and he was trying to teach the pup all he knew. I can remember watching Smoky, run through the dark green grass and the tall trees. He ran with the swiftness and assurance that came from knowing every foot of earth traveled over a million times, on those four short, stubby, little legs. His jet black hair glistened in the brilliance of the slowly fading sun. I could still see his sad little brown eyes which could touch even the coldest of hearts and see his eagerness to earn my approval by obeying my every comand. As long as I live, I'll never forget that black dog with the same appearance of any other dog, but the intelligence of a human being. I went to school and when I came home every day I looked for Smoky. I missed him so much and walking up the hill I got this awful feeling and I knew he was dead because he never would have missed one day meeting me at the bus stop. I could not help it, the tears started comming and I thought they weren't going to quit.

My mom said everything has to die sometime.

"Why did it have to be my dog?"

My mom said she thought humans were cruler than

12

animals. She said, she could not stand to see an
animal killed.

Years later, we found out Mr. Clayton killed
Smoky. Just before Mr. Clayton died he talked with
this guy, who was a friend of ours. This guy came
and told us that the old man said killing Smoky
was about the only thing he was sorry he did. He
died alone in his old shack on the hill.

I hated school more and more and I just could
not keep out of trouble. I liked some of the things
they told you, like the stories with happy endings
and how everybody should be nice. They put me in
all the dumb groups and the teacher said I was
lazy. I weighted 145 lbs. and was 5 ft. 4 in. tall,
in the fourth grade and I was fatty, fatty, two
by four that could not get through the kitchen
door. I kept sluging boys in the mouth and getting
sent to the office.

I collected copper wire and all kinds of metal
and old things that were just lieing around and
the junk man came and give me $5.00, the most mo-
ney I ever had. When mom went to town that week
I went in the store and bought a bunch of stuff,
arrows, marbles, candy, and funny books. My dad
collected junk and sometimes got forty or fifty
dollars.

My dad came home from work and he was really
mad, I thought I probably did something until he
started talking. "Do you know who that old s.o.b.
is lettin' move in here?"

"What are you talkin' about?" ask my mom.

"Old Vic is lettin' some god dam niggers move
in."

"What's a nigger, daddy?" ask my little sister.

"Oh shit, there black s.o.b.'s." My dad kept
on yelling and drinking his wine. "We ought to
get up a klu klux klan, and run them out."

Finally he went to bed. The next day my little
sister and I were hiding behind a tree watching
our new neighbors move in.

"Kerry we better stay behind this tree and

13

watch them because no telling what nigger people are like."

There was a chicken coop right by the tree and a tall, thin black man started walking toward it, when he saw my sister and I. I was about ready to run when I heard him say to his wife, who was standing on the steps of there house, "Honey, get some candy for these chillens."

I told Kerry to let me look at the candy first because it might be poison. The man came over to us and he had such a soft voice and his eyes were so kind. He stood there and then his wife came over and gave us some candy. His wife had the biggest smile I ever saw and she was big and soft looking and her eyes were shiny and happy. That was the first time I ever saw Odessa and her husband. My mom and Odessa became very good friends and she would go to town with us and those were my favorite times because my mom and her would always laugh and she would always be so nice to Kerry and I.

Kerry and I would go over to Odessa's house every chance we got. Her house was so warm and she would give us candy and let us watch her t.v. She was always laughing and my mom would come over and watch Kate Smith Show, that was her favorite show and Odessa and her would play cards, my mom was so happy. Odessa seemed to make everything and everybody smile and she could look at you and sometimes I thought she knew everything inside me and things did not hurt so bad. I loved her very much and she gave my mom two carved elephants and all kinds of nice things when she moved. She was a singer in a night club and she had a beautiful voice.

One night my dad started cussing and saying things about Odessa and it hurt so bad to hear him saying those awful things about her.

"Mama how can he say those things about Odessa?"

"I don't know why that old fool does anything."

One day we were playing cards, Odessa use to

14

let me and Kerry play cards. I was counting and
going enie menie, minie mo, when I said nigger
and I wanted to die. Odessa just looked me in
the eyes and I knew she knew I did not do it on
purpose.

The day Odessa moved and I kissed her good
by, it was the last time I saw her. My mom told
me when she died, and how she died of cancer.

I went to my valley and dreamed and sit by
a tree and looked at the sky and watched the
wind blowing through the grass, the grass swaded
and the wind hummed, it was so beautiful there
and there was nothing but sweet memories of
love and happiness there.

I often thought of Odessa, sometimes I remembered Smokey running through the hills but
most of all I remembered two years of happiness before I met Odessa. In that valley with
Shirley my first love, a girl with long curly
hair and a smile, she was gone and I tryed not
to think about it. When she left my mom said
she didn't like us any more.

Chapter Three

In the mornings before I
went to school, or when
I came home from school,
my mom and I would talk.
I can remember sitting
on our couch and listen-
ing to her. She would be
cleaning or sewing. It
seemed like she was al-
ways doing something.
"Sharon, you are going
to have to learn to have
some guts! You are going to have to learn that
this is a hard life, and no one gives a dam whether you sink or swim. You have to learn to stick
up for your self and not let people run over you."

"I don't let no one run over me mom."

"You and Kerry think you have it so bad. Well,
I want to tell you, you don't know what bad is.
I'll never forget when we lived up in the hills
in Wyoming, that was between nineteen thirty and
thirty six, when we lived in this house in the
winter, it was a brown shingle house. In the summer we lived on the homestead; the homestead was
our summer place, and it was a log cabin. There
was rats a foot long in both houses, we use to
get clubs and kill them. This couple that had a
new born baby and lived about thirty miles away
from us found a rat in their babies crib and the
rat had eaten half the babies head. They killed
the rat but the baby was dead. That same winter
we ran out of food, and had to live on frozen
potatoes. Another family froze to death. That was
a real bad year."

"We use to wake up in the morning, and break
the ice off the pale of water we used for drinking and left in the kitchen. Then we would put
some logs in the wood stove. It use to get thirty
and forty below zero in the winters. We also had
to melt snow on a wood stove for washing, taking

baths and drinking water. We had to have enough
wood and food for the whole winter. We bought
flour, salt, potatos, lard, beans and sugar, but
your dad got a few conttontail rabbits in the
winter. The snow would cover the house and we
would dig a hole through it to get out. Your dad
had a rope tied from the house to the barn so he
could get there to feed the cows and sheep without being lost when there was a blizzard."

"I washed my clothes on a washboard and in the
summer carried the water in from the well. I made
all my bread and milked the cow for milk and made
butter, cottage cheese and ice cream. I had a
garden in the summer for vegetables. There was no
electric lights, we used coal oil lamps. We had
a out house, but in the winter and at night in
the summer, we used the iron pot we had. We had
no ice box and in the summer we hung our food in
the well. We were snowed in for six months at a
time. Your dad made snow shoes and skis so he
could get to his trap lines to check them. You
could not use a horse or anything but snow shoes,
skis, or a home made sled, because of the snow
drifts. He trapped badgers, fox, and racoons for
their furs, then when we went to Wheatland, after the snow melted, he sold them. We went to
town about twice a year, we bought the kids oranges and apples. They only saw oranges or apples
when we went to town and they liked them better
than rock candy. Back there you had no fruits
or nuts except when it was certain seasons."

"This one time your sister Billie got food
poisoning from some lunch meat we bought and we
had to leave her in town. Your grandma, the old
bitch, had to take your sister in. I told that
doctor not to take Billie over there but he did
any way. She pushed Billie down and split her
lip open and when Billie called her grandma, she
said, "Don't call me grandma you little s.o.b."
She just up and put Billie out in the street
and a good thing a neighbor was around to take
Billie in. That old bitch was the biggest hel-

17

lion I ever seen and your dad runnin over there
to give her money when she did that to his kid,
besides the fact we didn't have a dam thing." My
mom's eyes were wild and I could feel the hate
she felt for that old woman and I knew it was true
what she said, but I did not like to see my mom
so upset. My mom never cussed eccept when she
talked about grandma.

"That old bitch put your dad out to work like
a man at age 12. He was workin on the railroad
splitting rails. She sold her daughter to an old
man for a loaf of bread. Your grandad use to hit
your dad with a two by four and they used to take
every cent he made. They went to church every
Sunday, the god dam hypocrites. That old bag runnin' to church and she would steal pennies off a
dead man's eyes. I use to be a lilly liver and
take shit, but I'm not takin' anything off anyone any more. Your dad runnin' over there ballin'
like a big baby while she cussed him. He would
run out and get drunk or steal something to get
even with god, for being so rottin' to his ma,
when she sit and told him her sad story or talked about bein' so bad off. She is so tight, she
probably has more money than we'll ever see."

"You can lock a theif out of your house, but
not a lier. All that old bag does is lie and
cheat and use her kids. She made our lives hell
and your dad will never quit kissin' her butt."

"We had a herd of sheep that your dad took
care of and in the summer at the homestead, your
dad use to sheer and butcher them. To this day
I can't stand mutten. These two old sheep herd-
ers come around and wanted to buy our dog, because it was the best sheep dog around and when
we would not sell teddy they slipped in one night
and stole him. About a week later he come back
with his paws worn to where there was no pads on
them. He ran away from thoes sheepherders and
must of walked miles to get home. The kids use
to pour water in gopher holes and then when the
gophers ran out of the holes, teddy used to grab
18

them and shake their guts out. The kids used to
scream and say sik'em. That dog was really smart."

"This one time Jimmy wanted to ride this calf
and your dad put him on and the calf bucked and
bucked and Jimmy landed on the ground and had a
bloody nose. He got up and screamed at the top of
his lungs, "I don't want to be a God dam cowboy,
I want to be a sheepherder."

"We came to California in nineteen thirty six.
We came out in a model A. We camped along the
roads at night or slept in the car. In the day we
would have to get out of the car going up hills
and push. They didn't have paved roads in those
days. They were asphalt or dirt roads and we would
go along and run over a chuck hole and everyone
would bump there heads on the top of the car. We
got to California and stayed with my sister, your
aunt Golda, until your dad got a job. Then we
lived in one shack after another. We've lived in
some of the worst holes you ever saw. I been
stuck in some hole all my life with a bunch of
kids. Then every time I go anywhere, your dad
starts drinkin' and fightin' until we have to
come home. We can't go anywhere. Your dad never
even had a childhood. He lived a dogs life with
that old woman. That's pretty awful not even being able to have a childhood."

"I'm sorry mom, I know I'm lucky."

"I'm tellin' you Sharon, you got to get some
guts or you're never going to make it!"

My dad usually talked to me when he had been
drinking, or at the dinner table. My mom used
to get mad at me because she said I always wreck-
ed dinner. There usually was a big fight. She
said, I always got my dad to yellin' by tellin'
him stuff and askin' him fool questions.

"Sharon, I can remember when I was nine years
old that was the first time I got put in jail.
That's one thing, kid, you don't ever want to
mess with the law. Well, this kid got a new bi-
cycle and had it parked outside of his house.
Well, I thought I would go for a little ride, so

I was gone for three hours. When I got back they
had called the sheriff on me. I spent the night
in jail. Before I married your ma, I was runnin'
a still up in the hills and makin' corn whiskey.
Those were the days of prohibition and it was a-
gainst the law to drink. That was one of the happiest days of my life when they got rid of that
God dam law. Well, me and these guys used to make
and run this whiskey and this one time the revenuers came up in the hills, huntin' all the stills.
They caught me, but I gave them a good run for
their money. Them s.o.b.s chased us all over those
hills. We had just finished makin' a big batch of
corn whiskey, too, and those God dam revenuers
probably had a dam good time with that whiskey.
They were probably drunk for a month. Any way,
them dam jails are the worst places and after me
spending half my time in'em when I was a kid, I
decided to never mess with the law. I ain't been
in no jails since I was married to your ma."

"When I was young I had a build on me, and
would work out every day on those bars I made out
of, two by fours and pipe. I used to ride buck-
ing bronks in the rodeo, and that was where I
messed up my voice from screamin' at those god
dam rodeos. I did some professional fighting, too
and I was really a tough s.o.b. Your ma is always
gettin' mad at me for fightin', but I ain't gonna
let no s.o.b. run over me. I've layed away many
big s.o.b.s that thought they were tough. Sharon,
I'm gonna tell you somethin'. If you ever come
home and tell me you lost a fight, I'm gonna
beat the shit out of you."

"Your brother Bob was really some kid. When he
was nine he could beat up any kid between nine
and eighteen in the neighborhood. That little shit
was the toughest kid I ever seen. Hell, he would-
n't back away from anything. And work, that kid
could outwork alot of men. He would chop wood and
sell it and any other job he could get he'd do."

"You kids ought to be dam glad you got parents
that give a dam about you. Your ma and me never

20

had anyone give a dam about us. When we were married we spent the first week we was married in a
barn. When your ma had Billie no one would help
us or nothin! We were drivin' along this road into town just before your ma had Billie and we got
stuck in a snow drift. We had to walk twenty
miles in thirty below weather, and we almost did-
n't make it. I really thought your ma was a gon-
ner, she kept wantin to lay down, and go to sleep,
and my hands got frostbit. Well no one even give
a dam, we could of layed out there and died, and
no one would even give a dam."

"I don't care what any of my kids did, even if
they murdered someone, no one better try and do
nothin to'em around me. I don't care what you do,
you're my kid."

Bob and Jim

"Most people don't give a dam about their kids. They just let them run wild, and never care about them. They don't teach kids nothin' either. Kids go around screamin' and yellin' and don't know enough to come in out of the rain. Those god dam teachers are nothin' but a bunch of queers. They don't know nothin' either. I ain't never seen a teacher that could even do a day's work. I'm talkin' about a man that would do a woman's work. Those men teachers are just queers. I ain't got no use for them. They don't even make any money at teachin! I never seen anyone with a college education yet that was worth a dam. Half of'em starve to death. There ain't nothin' worse than a god dam queer."

"Sharon, if anyone says anything to you knock'em down, and be god dam glad you ain't no runt."

Mom said, "I'm tellin' you Sharon, you got to get some guts or you're never going to make it."

I don't know what to do. I'm always getting in trouble. I know I'm lucky, but I do not understand.

We were going to move. I did not want to go and leave my valley. I did not like to think about going to a strange place. I was afraid. My mom was happy to be moving so she would not have to be worrying about the dirt and she was getting a new house. My dad got a new job working for a construction company in Concord.

Chapter Four

We were moving and ev-
eryone seemed very hap-
py. My mom could do her
wash any time she wanted
and not worry about the
dust and dirt. She was
close to the stores, and
the new house was larger.
This was the nicest place
my mom had ever lived in
and I was really glad to
see her happy. My dad had

a new job working for a construction company in
Concord and he would be getting more money and
that would help also. My brother Bob joined the
Navy and had left for San Diego, to enter boot
camp. A couple of days after he left, some Army
m.p.s came looking for him. My mom told them he
was in the Navy, but they did not believe her.
They said, Bob was a draft dogger. I guess they
finally received some proof that Bob was not a
draft dogger.

As we drove away from the mines I looked at
the mountains and I remembered Smoky and I running through the hills and the freedom and happiness I had felt. I knew I was leaving something
behind and I felt like yelling stop, stop, I do
not want to leave, but I did not say anything. I
sat there in the car and this empty quietness was
inside of me, I was no longer free, I no longer
felt like I was anything.

The new house was nice and my mom and dad
started planting flowers and shrubbery around our
flat top house. Our neighborhood was a housing
tract on the outside of Martinez, California. I
thought the tract looked like rows of boxes, neatly layed out street by street, with green and
brown touches of personality to try and prove they
weren't all the same. I did not like living there,
everywhere I walked there were no trespassing

signs. I had no where to go and I felt lost, without my valley and the birds, deer and all the
things I loved. I met some boys and started playing football and baseball and I felt better. Then
one day my mom and dad said, "Sharon, your getting too big to be playing with the boys, it does-
n't look right."

I thought, I don't give a dam what looks right,
I want to play football.

My sister in law came over to visit and she
and my mom bought me a bra. I felt like taking
that bra and ripping it apart, I hated it.

"Sharon, your getting to be a young lady and
you have to act and look like one."

"Junes right, Sharon, your a young lady now."

"Mom do I have to ware this thing?"

"Yes, Sharon you are going to have to start
acting right too and you can't play any more football or act so awful any more. I tryed to tell you
this before but you would not listen and the old
man kept encouraging you."

O.k. I thought, I guess I have to give up everything and be a stinken young lady, but that does
not mean I have to like it and no body seems to
care what I like or want. You have to look right
and do what people think you should. I think I hate
everyone. Why do I have to give up everything I
love? Why is it wrong for me to be what I want to
be? I guess I must be a awful person. I guess I
don't care about anything, anymore.

I can remember walking around going to school
and living from day to day, but I felt so lost
and this sad feeling I felt inside would not go
away. I did not know what was happening to me and
I wished someone would make that sad feeling go
away.

One day after school, my mom, Kerry and I, went
with a neighbor to Oakland. Kerry and I were very
impressed because all the buildings were so large
and there were so many people walking on the streets.
I was also frightened because I never saw so many
people. There was also traffic all around us and

24

I admired Lucille for being able to drive in the
traffic. We went to the salvation army store. Mom
said, she hoped no one found out about it. Mom
bought me a dress. I ask her and Lucille what I
was supose to say if someone ask me where I got
the dress. Mom said, "Just tell them you got your
dress at Sallys, an expensive women's store in
Oakland." Then they started laughing. I thought
we would all die from laughing so hard.

The next day when I wore the dress to school,
I did not feel much like laughing. I felt very
confused because I did not know how to feel about
that dress. I was afraid someone would find out
and I also thought it was funny and I also felt
sorry for myself.

At that time too, I could not figure out whether I was rich or poor. I did not have fancy
clothes like some of the girls, but I did not
like fancy clothes. Where we lived was supose to
be where the tough kids lived and no one seemed
to think it was a very good neighborhood. I did
not understand, because it was the nicest house
we ever had and my dad said, it cost $8,000 and
it would take him twenty years to pay it off.
Well, that seemed like alot of money to me.

When the other kids bragged about their houses
I bragged about mine, but that made me sad inside.
Why was I sad? I really do not understand how I
feel, what makes me feel this way or what makes
me feel that way or why? I just kept getting more
and more confused.

Then one day at school this girl came up and
said, "Hay, I bet you a coke I can throw a football further than you."

"O.k."

Well, she lost a coke, because she sure could
not throw the football further than me. That was
the first time I met Janice and I liked her from
the very start. I thought Jan was beautiful. She
had long brown hair, that had sun streaks in it,
and she had proxide on the front of her hair and
it looked really nice. Proxide on the front of

25

your hair was the fad. She had large brown eyes,
that sparkled with mischief. She had a good shape
but she was about ten lbs. over weight. She was
always being kided about her size 38 chest. I
started running around with Janice and she told
me what to wear and how to wear it.

"Sharon, you have to learn what color goes with
what. Never wear green and blue or pink and red.
You just have to quit wearing stripes with prints.
This is going to take alot of work. Your going to
have to call me at night so I can tell you what
to wear. Your going to have to get some tight
skirts and sweaters and white oxfords with long
shoe strings."

This was the year of 1954 and 1955.

Well when my mom took me to buy my school
clothes I did what Janice said. My mom got me
three tight skirts and two sweaters and two blou-
ses. I also got a pare of white oxfords and 64
inch shoe strings. I got a pare of levis and my
dad gave me a couple of his old white shirts. My
mom said, she thought all the kids looked silly,
the way they dressed. She said, at least I was
interested now, when before I would not even help
her pick out my clothes. I also got my next door
neighbor, Mrs. Perry to give me a D.A. hair cut.
Janice showed me how to comb my hair, and I learned some hep talk, man, go man go, daddio, clean,
boss, also a new singer was just starting out El-
vis Presley.

Janice was really smart and she seemed to know
everything. We could play baseball and catch and
ride bicycles and there was nothing wrong with it.
That made me happy, but I could not understand
how she knew how to get to do everything without
getting in trouble or getting laughed at. Oh well,
I was feeling happy and I sure was lucky to have
a friend like Janice. Janice was always joking
and everybody liked her. I never talked, because
I had to much fun listening and also I knew if I
opened my mouth something wrong always came out.
I always said, "What ever you want to do Jan, or

26

I don't care." Janice use to get mad sometimes,
but then I would give a suggestion and everything
was o.k. I was always happy when I was with Janice, but when I went home I was unhappy. My dad
was always telling me what to do.

My mom and dad did not like Janice and tryed
to make me stop running around with her. I was
not going to quit running around with Janice and
I did not care what they said, or did. My dad was
always giving me a bad time. Don't slam the door,
don't walk like that, you make to much noise. Don't
sit that way. I had to be home before he got home
from work. I could not go outside after dark. I
could only have one glass of milk, if I spilled
it I got slaped in the mouth. I hated dinner time
more than anything else. There was always a fight
or I would get slaped in the mouth or dad would
be drunk and start yelling and cussing. I could
not have kids over to our house, I could not spend
the night with anyone. I had to go to bed at 9:00
p.m. I could not leave lights on that were not being used. Had to use only two sheets of toilet paper. I had to follow these rules and a dozen more
until I was eighteen and left home.

I'll never forget the day I started Junior
High, I was scared. When we walked in the building these kids were standing in the hall and they
really looked tough. It reminds me of the movie
blackboard jungle. All the new kids were supose
to get hazed, but no one touched Jan and I. Janice said, "Don't act like your scared and if they
say anything to you just look right in there eyes
as mean as you can." I was not afraid of being
beat up, because I was a good fighter but I was
afraid of everything being so strange. Janice and
I worked as a team, I was the muscle and she was
the brains. Janice was also a pretty good fighter
too.

No one bothered us and Janice told jokes and
talked to all the kids and pretty soon we knew
all the kids. We laughed and had a good time. All
the kids that were our friends, were supose to be

27

the bad kids in the school, but they were not bad.
We did not care what anyone said. Janice, Carol,
Val, Helen and me ran around together. This one
day on our lunch hour we walked to town to buy our
lunch. We passed this funeral parlar and there was
this guy painting the outside of it. Well, Janice
said, "Hay Mr. you got any dead bodies in there
that we can look at?"

"Ya, Miss. Lucy is in there you can take a look
if you want, but don't stay in there because her
family will be here pretty soon."

We went in the funeral parlar and looked at the
dead body. I did not like that and I felt sick
and they all laughed. Then we had to get back to
school. Well, we were late, so we all had to go
to the office. They ask me what happened and I
did not say anything. They called the other girls
in and said I told everything so then the girls
talked. The girls dean said I was the worst one
of the bunch and at least the other girls con-
fessed. She also said it was very desrespectful
for us to look at Miss Lucys body, because it
would be like making fun of the dead. Well, we
were real respectful and did not laugh until we
got out side and not at Miss Lucy, but because
that was a weird experience.

Janice and I were smoking and she said, she
learned to inhaile. She showed me how to inhaile
and it made me sick and dizzy. I did not want to
smoke, because I did not like it, but I was not
chicken. To be chicken was to lose all your
friends and you would be laughed out of school.
All of us kids would stand around smoking all
the time and everybody thought we were really
bad. Men and women would stare at us and Janice would stick her tongue out at them and we
would laugh and laugh. One morning we were having a cigarette and Janice said, "Hay lets pick
our teacher some flowers."

So we picked these two big bouquets of flowers and we gave them to our teachers. The teachers thought something was up, when Jan and I

gave them the flowers. They started asking us
questions and finally we landed in the office.
We had to go and tell the lady that owned the
flowers we were sorry for picking her flowers
and got in all kinds of trouble.

Carol and Val started running around with
their boy friends. They use to just walk around
holding hands and before you knew it everyone
was saying they were whores. Well, if anyone
said anything in front of us they would sure
get it because we knew Carol and Val were not
whores. Carol came to school with bruses all o-
ver her and we found out her dad beat her and
raped her. No one give a dam about that, no one
would do anything about that, people could just
tell lies about people, but they did not really
care what was happening to my friends and what
hell they were living.

Janice, Helen and I got caught smoking and
were kicked out of school. I was really scared
and I did not want to go home. I walked in and
said, "Mom I got kicked out of school for smoking."

"You what! Your dads going to kill you. I
know who's fault this is, that dam Janice is
the cause of this. I don't want you going around
with her anymore."

"It was not Janice's fault it was mine, it
was my fault!"

"Your a stupid little fool, if she said, to
jump off a bridge you would do it."

"No! I wouldn't!"

"We're going to have to figure some way of
keeping your dad from finding out about this.
Your going to have to get up in the mornings
and pretend to go to school until he leaves for
work."

My mom could not stop me from seeing Janice
and I was not going to quit running around with
her. My mom did not care about me or anything
about how I felt. I hated my dads guts. He would
not let me do nothing and was always knocking me

29

around. I felt like I was closed in, in that house and I could not even open my mouth. I wished I could leave and never come back.

On our lunch hour we would walk to Martinez. Martinez was a small town owned by small businessmen. A lot of large companies wanted to move into Martinez, but no one would sell them land. So right today, Martinez is almost the same as when I was going to school. Martinez main street was only about twelve blocks from school and all the stores were on the main drag. We started shop lifting. I did not like stealing. If my mom would ever find out it would kill her. My mom thought stealing was an awful thing. She said, she would starve, before she would steal. Thou shalt not steal, she said, she would never break one of Gods comandments.

I really felt bad about stealing. Most of the time I did not steal anything. Janice and Helen got mad at me and called me a chicken, so I stold fifty cents worth or a dollars worth of stuff. Janice and Helen use to add up all they stold and they would at least get $20.00 a peace a day. Then we started stealing cigarettes and hard liquar, then we would sell it at school. Janice and Helen could steal anything, from water mellons to full can can slips. At school the girls dean was checking our lockers so we had to change our loot from one locker to another between every class.

My mom and dad let us sleep outside in sleeping bags. I about fainted, because my dad did not like kids over at the house and especially to spend the night. Anyway, we stold a fifth of vodka, so we could get drunk and just before we went to bed we walked up to the little store about two blocks away. Kerry had to come with us and Helen was going in and steal a bunch of goodies for us. Kerry said she wanted to go in the store with Helen.

"No! Kerry you stay here with Jan and I."

"I'm going in and I don't care what you say

Sharon."

Well when Helen and Kerry came out of the store Helen was laughing and Kerry was crying. Helen said she got caught and her and Kerry could not go back in the store. Helen laughed and said, she got caught but she still had 5 cup cakes and 4 pies on her that he did not find. Helen was a riot, she had long dark brown hair and was one of the thinest girls in school. She had dark brown eyes and a flawless olive complextion. Helen couldn't fight her way out of a paper bag, so she had to stay close to Jan and I or she would get beat up. Sometimes I thought Helen was kind of crazy. About ten years later we found out she was epileptic.

"Sharon, Helen is a stealer, a real stealer. What am I going to do if mama askes me to go to the store? Oh my mama's going to hate me, becaus of you low down stealers."

"I told you not to go in that store you little dumb bell."

We went back to the house, and then went out in the back yard. Kerry was still crying and we told her to take a drink of vodka. Kerry started giggling and acting stupid and then Jan went over by the dog house and was sitting there cross legged having a pow wow with Helen. Jan was also telling jokes, she said, "There was this hep cat and he was going to Cathlic school and the priest told him, it was bad enough when he called the fathers daddio and the sisters sis, but when he called Jesus Christ and his Disciples, J.C. and the gang, that was going too far." By this time I was getting worried because if my mom and dad came out they would know were were drinking. Finally I got them to lay down and go to sleep. Man, I did not have any fun that night. Also about three o'clock in the morning, when Jan, Helen and I were asleep, Kerry got up and went in the house and woke up my mom so she could confess, because her guilty conscience could not wait for morning.

31

The next day when we went in to breakfast my
mom cornered Helen and ask her about what happened. Helen talked her way out of it and my mom
still liked her. Kerrys eyes were all blood shot
from crying. I don't remember being like that at
age 12, or any other age, I was fourteen then
and we were in the eighth grade. The two years
of junior high seemed to be just flying by.

Jan, Helen, and I decided to have our own private club. We called our club the top notchers,
we got our long white mens shirts and put our em-
blem on them. JS We decided we should all put a
cigarette out on the back of our hand, to really
make it a club. I took a cigarette and put it
out on my hand and did not cry or make a sound.
Helen, screamed and was scared. Jan yelled and
her eyes watered. There was also a fad, where
you took a razor blade and cut your initials in
your arm. So we did that too. We wore our shirts
to school and when we walked down the hall everyone moved out of our way. Jan said, see I told
you. Even the roughtest kids in school were a-
fraid of us and we didn't have to do anything.

I really felt miserable. I wished I could
talk to someone and they could tell me what was
happening to me. If I only could tell someone
the way I really felt. I did not like what I was
doing, but even if I did not do anything I was
wrong. Why did life have to be this way? I felt
so alone inside, why couldn't there be someone
to help me, like in the movies. My parents did
not care about me and no matter what they said,
I knew deep down inside of me they did not love
me. Why didn't my parents love me, what did I
do? Oh shit, I don't care.

Chapter Five

We rode our bikes into
town and went in a mar-
ket and Helen and I
kept the clerk busy
while Jan rolled a wat-
er mellon out the door.
We had a problem tho,
how were we going to
cut the water mellon.
Jan saw a lady working
out in her yard and so
Jan went over to her
and said, "Hey, lady could we barrow a knife
from you to cut our water mellon?"

The lady was very nice and went in her house
and got us a knife. We ate all the water mellon
we could hold and then we decided that we could
not carry the rest of it home on our bikes. Jan
saw this big fancy car and went over and the
door was open, so we put the water mellon in it.

"Can't you see their faces when they get in
that car, their probably rich people. ha, that's
really a good joke."

"It sure is, a half ate water mellon in a paper bag in the front seat of a Cadillac, ha ha."

Jan and Helen were trying to teach me the bop,
the bop was a popular dance. Well, I had two left
feet and they were getting mad at me, because as
hard as they tryed, I still could not do the bop.

"Sharon, I never saw anyone as clumbsy as you
in my life!"

"I can't help it Jan, I never danced before."

"Well, you don't even have any rhythem, I never seen anyone that can't even keep time to the
music."

I never could listen to music, unless Billie
or Jim came over to visit, or we went to visit
them. Mom and dad did not like music. So all I
ever heard was, music from the fortys or early
fiftys, like Billie and Jim liked. The jitter

bug or the slow music Jim and Billie liked was
not popular, rock and roll was the music Jan and
everyone liked. If I said I liked "You belong to
me" by Jo Stafford or "Wheel of fortune" by Kay
Star, I would be square of the year. Wow, things
sure got complicated about the dumbest stuff.
Anyway, Jan and Helen finally gave up trying to
teach me to dance, it was a lost cause.

Janice did not know until they handed her,
her diploma if she was going to graduate from junior high. It was really awful and we were worried. I passed and did not try very hard and because of that they would not let me take any
classes in high school to prepare for college.
That really hurt me, when the girls dean said, I
was not smart enough to study to go to college.
I really wanted to study to go to college more
than anything. If I could go to college I would
be the first in my family. The girls dean signed
me up for a basic and general study in high
school. I should have tryed harder but now it
was to late. I think it made the dean happy to
put me in all the dumb classes. She gave us a
bad time all through junior high. Everytime something happened she would call Janice, Helen and
I to the office. Oh well, I did not give a dam
about anything. Everyone said, I had a rotten
attitude. Well, what was I supose to do anyway,
how did you do something about a attitude? What
was a bad attitude anyhow?

We talked all summer about high school. The
hazing in high school was worse than in junior
high, but Jan, Helen, and I had built quite a
reputation so we weren't worried about the hazing.

The first day of school was o.k. no one hazed
us and we really felt proud. In the mornings before school we would go to the store by the
school and buy cigarettes and cokes. Three more
kids joined our croud, Borgie, Carolyn and Gary.

Borgie was a riot, she was about 5'4 and heavy
set and was kind of homely, but she was alot of

34

fun. We sure did laugh at the way she smoked,
she would hold her cigarette up in the air like
a movie star and cross her legs and really looked dumb. She was really a good sport and laughed
about the way she smoked too.

Carolyn, was 5'7 and had blond hair and had
it cut in a d.a. She was a tom boy like the rest
of us, all but Helen. She sit around cracking
her nuckles all the time and never said to much
except that everything was dumb. No one ever bothered Carolyn either because she was really
tough. She was also a very sweet person that
would do anything for you if you were her friend.
Carolyn never would sign her name in our year
books, she always said that was stupid. She
learned how to write her name in our senior year.
She was in a speachal class for kids that could-
n't learn to read and write.

Gary, was really sweet and had a soft voice
and dressed very nice and his dad owned thee
store we went to every morning before school.
Gary use to help us steal stuff from his dads
store. I did not understand that, but Gary just
laughed and stold things too.

We had alot of fun smoking and stealing but I
knew it was not right and I thought we better
quit. I did not like talking nice to Gary's father and then stealing stuff from him. So, I
told Jan either they quit stealing or I would
quit running around with them. Jan said, "Who do
you think you are? As far as that goes, I don't
want to run around with you if you think you're
so dam good. You can't run around with us Sharon!"

Boy, I had a big mouth now I had no one to
run around with. Who, was I going to run around
with? Kathy, a very nice girl in one of my classes ask me to run around with her and two other
nice girls. They were girls from nice homes and
were studious. They weren't "white shoes" but
were close to it. They liked me and wanted to
help me. They weren't snobs or didn't look down
on people and they were going to help me talk

right and quit smoking. At first it was boring studying on lunch hour and being so nice but then I was beginning to like it except for not riding bikes or playing baseball and about some day getting married and having kids and being a housewife. Why would anyone want to be a house-wife if they could travel and see the world and go to college? I had been running around with Ka-thy for about a week when Val came up to me and called me over away from Kathy and the girls and said, "Sharon, what are you doing with thoes goodie, goodie, white shoes?"

"Val, their not white shoes, their nice."

"I'm not going to let you run around with peo-ple like that, come on!"

I did not know what to say. I think I said good by before Val grabbed me by the arm and lead me off.

"The white shoes" were kids whose fathers were the town society and businessmen, or ones that just plain had money. "The white shoes" ran all the school clubs, dances and offices. They wore nice clothes and knew the right things to say. I never could talk or express myself very well, especially if more than one person ap-proached me at a time. If two people started talking to me at once, like if they were mad at me, or asking me something I would get mixed up and couldn't speak. If someone asks me something where you have to be diplomatic I also sometimes can't talk. I know that sounds silly but thats what happens to me. Some people that are very good at talking can make me look stupid and all through my life, if there was someone like that within fifty miles, I would be unlucky enough to run into them, just so they could have some fun making me look stupid. Most of the time they were "white shoes" trying to put a lower person in there place.

"The black shoes" were the kids that were sup-posed to be tough and that smoked and said cuss words. Some of them were really hoodlums, but a lot of them weren't. Their family's didn't have much money. Their fathers were construction workers and general laborers. There were also the ones that were on welfare. I grew up with these kids and I always felt at ease with them. I never had any fear when I was in the company of so called ruff people because I could understand their feelings and thoughts. Val and Carol, were black shoes. They were also my two friends that went with Jan, Helen and I to the funeral parlor, we laughed about that remembering how much trouble we got into. I guess I did belong with them more than with Kathy. I don't know, maybe I did not belong anywhere because I did not exactly believe in to much of anything, it must be my rotten attitude.

All the black shoe girls run around together and all the boys ran around together. The groups mixed sometimes at lunch, or partys or if you were going steady with someone you went everywhere with them. Across the street from the school, was a store called the red and white. Everyone went there at lunch hour to smoke. The store was off the school boundries so you could not get kicked out of school for smoking there.

One morning we were at the red and white smoking, when we found out there was going to be a fight.

"Hay, Betty is going to fight some girl that called her a bitch."

There was about fifty or sixty kids waiting to see the fight. Betty brought her levis to school and had them on waiting for the girl. Her boy friend Kyle was waiting with her. "Here she comes Betty knock the hell out of her!"

The girl came walking up and Betty stood there smoking a cigarette and when the girl got in front of Betty, she fliped her cigarette in the girls face. Wow, they looked like wild cats clawing and rolling in the street. "Break her neck Betty!"

Jan, was there and she started directing the

37

traffic around the fight and everyone laughed.

"Look at that Jan directing thoes cars around, she's really funny."

Betty pulled a big chunk of the girls hair out with part of her scalp. Betty also bit a big hole in the girls leg. Someone said the cops were comming so everyone started to leave and the fight was broke up. Betty held the chunk of hair up in the air and yelled, "Me heep big fighter, me got scalp to hang on wall."

Carol ran away from home. Her dad was still beating her, she did not say how many times he raped her. She got put in Juvenile hall, (Juve), she said, when you went in there they gave you some kind of examination to see if you had sex. She said it really hurt. Three of the girls got caught shoplifting and went to the Juve and said, the same thing Carol said. It was really a awful place, crouded and besides if you went to the Juve the whole school would find out and then forget it, if you were a girl your reputation was gone. You had to take a blue slip to your classes saying you were in the Juve. At least the black shoes did not look at anyone like they were dirt for getting into trouble. I did not think it was right to make a person a outcast, or make them go through life being looked down on and called names because of a mistake or for being different. How could people sit around judging people? How come some people sitting some where could make it where a person went through the rest of there life being looked down on? Thoes rich goodie, goodie, people are the worst people in the world. Sitting there with there money, saying what is right and wrong. I bet if they lived here things would be different.

We use to see this boy and girl walking around all the time together and you could tell they were in love. She got pregnant and he moved away. She kept going to school and had her baby and kept it. All the girls thought she was really brave doing that. Everyone in school knew a-

bout it and kids use to be looking at her all
the time. She held her head up and finished
school. She was a very nice girl and all of us
admired her, it was really hard staying in school
with everyone talking about you.

Bunny and Donna were going with the two Hast-
ing brothers. All through school I never saw
much of Ron and Tommy because they were always
in reform school. They would never be out more
than a month at a time. Ron married bunny but
got killed by a cop. Tommy is in San Quinten
last time I heard. Bunny use to talk about Ron
all the time and how he was going to go straight
and they were going to get a house and settle
down. She was a very pretty girl, her hair was
cut in a poodle, a short tight hair cut that was
popular. I remember when I was going around with
the black shoes and Tommy got out of reform
school, they had a big party planned and the
night before him and three other boys robbed a
place and got sent up. All that day, thats all
anyone talked about.

There was going to be a big party in the trees.
The trees, were some trees outside of town on
some private property, away from a rode that did
not have to much traffic. There would be booze
and you were supose to bring a sleeping bag. We
planned everything for a week. I could not go because my dad did not let me go, if I did something like that and my mom found out it would
kill her. The way it turned out was no one spent
the night out there anyway, but they said it was
really alot of fun.

A new croud was getting together around our
neighborhood. About fifteen girls, and fifteen
boys, that were not black shoes or white shoes.
Jan, was in this group and she and I were friends
again.

Chapter Six

I hated money because everytime I wanted anything as long as I can remember, it cost my parents money. A coke cost so much, a candy bar cost so much. Mom had to really save to buy our clothes and when we went to school, the kids would say, "How come you wear the same thing all the time Sharon?" Or someone would look at me like I was from outer space. Christmas, and birthdays, I wished would never come. We would go to every sale in town and I did not like getting anything, because I knew how my mom had to go around from store to store. Those dam clerks would always look down there dam noses at my mom. My poor mom in a cheap house dress trying to do the best she could. I really hated those clerks guts, dressed nice and calling my mom, mame and acting like she was dirt under their feet. My mom would ask them in her soft quiet voice how much it cost and say she wanted the best, for the money she had. I hated to go in stores and it got so bad my mom had to threaten me to get me in a store. She had to pick out my clothes because I wouldn't, all I wanted to do was get out of there as fast as I could.

Some day I would get some money and pay back every cent it cost my mom and dad to raise me, I sware to god I will. I felt like some greedie louse. My mom would sit by the hour figering out the bills. She would tell me how much money they owed and she did not know if we could make it through the winter. In the winter my dad did not work much. Construction workers could not work in the rain and bad weather. So my mom had to save all the money, so we could live in the winter.

Everytime I ask for something, I knew how
hard my dad worked and there was not much money,
I felt really bad.

Some of the other kids had more than I did
and I wanted more but my mom had only three cotton dresses and my dad only had work clothes. I
hated myself for wanting more but I did not like
going to school and having kids look at me. I also felt bad when we had to tell what we got for
Christmas. My mom and dad never even got anything
for Christmas when they were young. My mom said
one Christmas she got a rag doll. I wanted to
cry, I hurt so bad inside. Bob, Billie, and Jim-
mie never got as much as we did, why was I always wanting more and feeling bad?

My dad would buy a cheap bottle of tokay or
muskatell wine and bring Kerry and I a coke. My
mom and dad would get in a big fight and then we
would have dinner, and my dad would pass out watching t.v. We had to go to bed at 9:00 every
night, except weekends.

One weekend Kerry and I went to the show and
we saw Barbara and Judy. They were best friends
and you never saw one without the other. They
were in my sixth grade class but I did not see
them much after grade school because they were
"white shoes."

I remember when I was in the sixth grade and
started my period. I ask Barbara if she started
ministrating yet?

"What's ministrating?"
"Forget it!"
"What is it Sharon?"
"Never mind, its not important."

The next day at school Barbara came up to me
and said, "My mom said, you ought to be suspended from school talking about menstruation! She
said she was going to the principal! Sharon,
your awful!"

Wow, was I scared. I really had a big mouth.
At recess a gang of boys came up to me and ask

41

me why did I upset Barbara with talk about administration? "Whats administration, Sharon?"

"Look, I don't know so leave me alone!"

That went on for about a week and I wished I was dead. I never thought I'd live through that mess. I did not want to get suspended either. I was so worried, but the principal never suspended me and everyone forgot about it. Every time I saw Barbara I thought of that and I never had a period for four years after that. To this day I only have a period once every four years. I don't know why.

That night at the show was the last time I saw Barbara because that night she died in her sleep, she had diabetes but knowone knew. Borgie and I went to her funeral. It was not the first funeral I ever went to. When I was about seven I remember my dad crying at his sisters funeral. Someone died every couple of years in my dad's family and he was always crying.

Everyone said, Barbara looked beautiful but I did not think that wax body laying there was pretty. I thought the person that use to be alive was pretty. They had to carry Judy out of the funeral parler because she was screaming and crying. The poll barers were the boys from our sixth grade class. Over half the student body was there and it was really sad. My mom was right when she said, "Sharon, the only hell is on earth."

Val, Carol, and I went to the show. We were waiting outside of the show for Val's mom to pick us up and these boys came up and started talking to us. Carol said she knew them and they were going to give us a ride home. I said I was not riding home with someone I did not know.

"Sharon, don't be a square, come on!"

Well, we ended up out parked in some feild. Carol and Val were making out with the other two boys. (Making out was prolonged kissing) I felt really stupid sitting there talking about cars with this boy, so when he started to kiss me I let him. I did not like kissing, it was differ-

42

ent than I thought it would be. He had wiskers
and I did not like that and I did not like his
big toung in my mouth. I sure thought it would
be different than that. I was glad when we left
but when we got to Val's house her mom was really mad, she saw us get out of the boys car."Your
starting out with boys this early hu?"

"I did not do anything wrong mom."

"Val, your not going to be a tramp, if I have
to beat you to death."

I was scared and so I backed out the door and
went home. I sure hope Val's mom don't tell my
parents. My dad would beat me to death.

A new croud was getting together and we use
to go over to Helen's house and watch american
bandstand a new show on t.v. One day my mom let
some of the kids come over to our house and make
home made ice cream. They never ate home made
ice cream and my mom explained how she use to
make butter and cottage cheese and all the other
things. We would go on hikes and swimming. Jan
never ran around with us much, she was always o-
ver at this girls house.

My brother Bob was out of the navy and living
over in Stockton with my brother Jim. He had a
girl friend and my mom and dad did not like it
because she had three kids, and the oldest was
same age as me. I'll never forget the night Bob
and Sue came over to our house. Mom and dad just
sat there watching t.v. and Sue was really ner-
vious. I felt so sorry for her. Finally she got
up real fast and went over to my mom and said,
"Mrs. Isabell, Bob and I are married."

Mom looked at the ring and then just kept on
watching t.v. and did not say a word. I had to
do something, I could not stand what was going
on, so I jumped up and tried to be real cheerful
and said, "Gee, I'm really glad your married,
congratulations."

Well, Bob and Sue sat there for a minute and
then left. I thought that was just awful and I
thought my mom and dad were really mean. I felt

so sorry for Sue, she was so little and my mom
and dad were not very nice to her.

Bob and Sue ask me to spend the weekend with
them. They were living in Stockton in Sue's house
and Bob was having a hard time finding a job. Sue
introduced me to her daughter Charmaine, and her
friend Gerene. I liked them right off and we
started talking. They were really square but they
were nice. We went over to Gerene's house and
while we were walking over there she told me a-
bout being adopted and that her mom was a teacher. She also said her mom had put her on a diet.
She weighted 190, and when we got in her bedroom
she reached under her mattress and pulled out a
box of candy. We laughed and ate some candy. We
started talking about boys and they came off
with something, that almost make me laugh. "Sharon, Gerene and I believe that you should never
kiss a boy on the first date, except until he
says good night and then the kiss will be his reward for such a nice date."

I was afraid to tell them about kissing that
boy, they would probably think I was a tramp.
People sure are different. I had a nice time and
Charmaine and I were friends for life.

My dad bought a boat so he could go fishing
and my brother learned to water ski and was teaching me. Water skiing was more fun than anything,
my mom did not like it because my dad would always get drunk. I sure liked to water ski, being
outside and flying across the water. You got the
most wonderful free feeling. My mom was really
mad about my dad buying the boat, she said, we
could not afford it and dad was crazy.

"You gota have some fun, shut your dam mouth."

"Look, you old fool, were not rich!"

"I'm keepin the boat, so you might as well
get use to it."

I was suppose to be in the school band but my
mom could not take me to school early so I had
to quit. I played in the band for last year's
graduating class and I was so proud wearing the
44

band uniform. The first day of my sophmore year
I quit the band, wow, I hated that. I gave the
school back their clarinet.

One of the biggest honers in school was to
have a letter sweater. All of us decided to get
our parents to take turns picking us up from
school, so we could stay after school and play
ball to earn our letter sweaters. Jan said,
some day before we graduate we'll win the badmitten trophy. That was really a dream, and
hard to think of as real.

All of a sudden kids were saying, "Sharon
your cute and you know it hu?"

"You got a cute shape Sharon."

Why, were they saying that, I was still me
and I did not like anyone saying that stuff.
That really embarrassed me, I hated that and
felt weird. This growing up stuff was getting
on my nerves.

Janice, Helen and I started cutting school.
We would buy cigarettes and steal some hot dogs
or something from the store and go over to Jan's
house because her mom worked and knowone was
home. This one day we wanted to have some hot
dogs but did not have any bread. I walked over
to my house and sneeked up the drive way. I looked in the house and my mom was in the back bedroom. So I sliped in and grabed a half of a loaf
of bread. When I came out, the door made a sound
and my mom came in from the bedroom. I hid behind
the boat and she did not see me. I went back o-
ver to Jan's house and we laughed and laughed.
Then the phone rang and we were scared. Jan ans-
wered it and someone hang up. The phone rang a-
gain and the same thing happened. We were really
getting scared when the phone rang again, this
time a voice said, "You dam brats cut school
didn't you? Tell Sharon if she don't get over
here I'll come over there and get her."

My mom was really mad and she said I could
spend the rest of the day helping her do house
work. She said, when she went in to fix her some

45

toast and the bread was missing and then just a
while before she heard a noise in the kitchen, so
she sat down and figured out, it must have been
me and that we had cut school. She knew Jan's
mom worked so she knew we were there, so she thought she would teach us a lesson. "You three think
your so smart, well your not!"

A notice came out at school, wanting new mem-
bers for a club called junior stateman.

"Let's join, and see whats it's about."

"Do you think you can join a club, there all
run by white shoes," Janice kept saying.

"Sharon, let's go to a meeting and see o.k?"

"O.k. Helen, I'll go."

We went to the meeting and there was some
white shoes there but they acted pretty nice. The
club was about politics and you would go to con-
ventions and learn about how the government was
run. There was going to be a state convention and
it would be in Sacromento, and some delagates
from our school would be in the state congress.
We would debate over bills in the capital just
like real state congress. Just think it would be
a weekend in Sacromento sitting in the capital
of our state making legislation and staying in
the Sentor hotel. I could see George Washington
and Abraham Lincoln, and think of all the great
things about freedom and I was going to be a
part of it. This club ment more to me than anything, just think of me Sharon Isabell apart of
freedom and justice for all. I was going to be
so good and really act right if it killed me.

If Helen and I could get fifteen dollars a-
peace we could go to the state convention. Well,
we were going to get it, so we started washing
cars and mowing lawns and I did all my mom's ironing and believe it or not we got the money. I
could hardly believe it. I took my eighth grade
graduation dress because there was going to be
a ball. Could you believe me and Helen at a ball
in the Sentor hotel in Sacromento, and a part of
the congress of the United States of America?

46

There I sat in a seat that a real Congressman had sat in. I never was so proud in my life. I sat there and my heart was beating and listened to the legislation and looked at the flag. My country was the greatest in the world, and the bills that were written at that convention were written by the kids that were there. Soon as I got home I was going to write a bill, I would really think of something good.

I thought Socialized Medicine would be one of the best things that could help the people. My mom and dad would have to barrow money from the bank and go deeply into debt if one of us had to go to the doctor or hospital. If we had Socialized Medicine it would help the poor, and actually give them more money, to spend in their every day life. Believe it or not I got into more arguments over that and my mom and dad, did not understand and thought I was just still the big mouthed kid.

Capital Punishment was something I disliked more than anything. It seemed so barbaric to want to kill a person, instead of useing our knowledge to try and descover or scearch for answers to find out what makes a person murder and the prevention. Also to find some way these people could be useful in working toward finding answers.

"If someone killed your parents wouldn't you want them dead?"

"The only reason everybody don't kill when they want to is because they don't want to go to the gas chamber."

"It would cost to much money to support those murders, who wants to put tax money toward keeping murders alive?"

A murder is a human being and to kill them seemed just as bad to me as when they killed someone. You kill someone, I'll kill you. We could figure out how to split a atom but we could not figure out or even want to figure out and help prevent killing period. Thou shalt not kill.

I could not stop thinking about the bills and

47

how the Lt. Governor spoke and said we were fine
young statesmen and welcomed us to the capital.
That night we had a big dinner and I was really
scared. I only ate in a drive-in-restaurant once
in my life. They had all these forks and everything was so strange. I really felt sick. I made
it through the dinner and then there was the ball.
All the kids were dressed up in these real fancy
clothes. I wanted to go and stay in my room but
Helen said she wanted to go to the ball. Then
some boy ask me to dance and I said no and Helen
pushed me out on the floor. I couldn't dance,
that was really rotten of her and I steped all
over the boys feet. We quit danceing and then he
kept standing there and I did not know what to
talk about. Then Helen wispered in my ear, "You
got a boy friend don't you?"

I felt like sluging her right there. I would
really be glad when it was all over. It's too
bad you had to go through dinner and a ball and
just couldn't talk about legislation, and interesting things.

I wrote a bill for the next convention. It was
just a one day convention but it was important
and I was really going to be proud when my bill
was brought up. My bill was on direct vote by the
people and abolishment of the electro college.
In the election between Tilden and Hayes in 1877
the popular vote was for Tilden. Hayes was elec-
ted by the electro college. This could happen a-
gain. If we abolished the Electro College by direct vote this, I believe, would prevent the popular vote from being taken advantage of. I really thought my ideas were important and I wanted
my bill to go before the next convention more
than anything.

A special meeting was called so we could
change the club rule about having to have a B av-
arage to be in the club. The teacher said, that
someone said, the rules of the club had to be
lived up to, so if we wanted to stay in the club
we had to change the rule. About fifteen white

shoes came to the meeting to vote us out. They had the majority so I made a speech.

"Please don't vote against changing the rule from a B to a C. We really want to stay in this club and we might smoke but when we go the convention we act nice. I have a bill I have just written to send to the next convention. We really believe in this club and we have really tried hard.

The teacher said, "I don't see how they can vote against you after that speech."

Well the teacher was wrong. They voted us out of the club and that was the end of the club. They didn't want it but they did not want us to have it. I hated ever one of their lillie white guts! Janice was right!

Kerry told a neighbor lady about me being in junior statemen before we got run out. The lady belonged to the Toastmistresses club in Oakland. Her husband was a toastmaster. She ask me if I would like to go with her and speak at one of the meetings. I said o.k. but I did not know what the Toastmistress was. The lady was a common person and I did not know about her husbands social background. Wow, when I saw the big building and walked into a group of women that had fur coats, I was scared to death. I was introduced and then I got up and tried to speak as nice as I could. The Chairman got up after I spoke and said, I was a very poised young lady and it was encouraging to know that young people were interested in government. I told Janice about the whole thing and she was in journalism class, so she told them and I got a whole article written about me in the paper.

I also wrote a book, it took me about five months but I wrote it. It was a mystery. My mom and dad thought I was crazy but I really finished my book. I kept it hid and some day I was going to publish it.

49

Chapter Seven

Our next door neigh-
bor's sister came to
visit her. Reatha was
nineteen, and had just
gotten a divorce. She
and I became friends,
but my dad did not like
me being friends with
Reatha. "I don't want
no daughter of mine run-
ning around with some
woman thats been mar-
ried. No tellin what she'll say."

Well, I still went over to talk to Reatha and
I did not care what he said, he did not like me
to do nothing.

It was a saterday, and I went over to talk to
Reatha. She ask me to read this true story maga-
zine. The story was about this lesbian and how
she felt about this girl. Everything the girl in
the story felt, I had felt. I felt scared and happy at the same time. Becomming aware of something
that you had kept so deep inside of you and did
not understand, was really strange. When Jan had
kissed me on the neck, just kidding around, I
felt funny all over, I had pretended it never happened. Now when I thought of her soft mouth and
the warmth of her closeness I knew my feelings
and other memories rushed into my mind. I knew my
secret but I did not know what to think, I was
confused.

"What did you think about that story, about
the lesbian, Sharon?"

"I don't know."

"Do you know what? My sister-in-law said, her
and her husband went to this bar and this lesbian
came over and just sat at there table. Then she
reached under the table and put her hand on my
sister-in-law's leg. Well, her husband jumped up
and was going to knock the hell out of that queer.

So you know, that queer pulled a knife on him.
Well, the men in that place just got a hold of
her and threw her out. My sister-in-law said, 'Women like that ought to be put away.' Do you know
what's wrong with them?"
    "What?"
    "Well, they got their passion in their throat."
    "Whats that mean?"
    "Well, instead of having it where your supose
to." (She shook her bottom part of her body) "They
got theirs in their throat."
    "How could they have that, in their throat?"
    "Well, I don't quite know, but they do. Their
freaks of some kind. Do you know what I think?"
    "What?"
    "You know your friend Jan?"
    "Ya, what about her?"
    "Well, when you introduced me to her she shook
my hand."
    "So?"
    "Well, thats one of the signs."
    "What do you mean signs?"
    "Well, how many women shake hands like men do?"
    "I don't know."
    "Well, not very many and I know how we can
find out if she is one. At the party tonight if
she don't make out with any of the boys we'll
know it for sure."
    "Jan always kisses the boys and they say she
makes out better than anyone."
    "That's that throat passion. Sharon, if I were
you, I would stay away from her because she might
turn you that way. You know they can make people
like that."
    June, Jims wife said she could get me a job
working at the hospital where she worked for the
summer. I said, I would like to get a job to buy
my school clothes. So, I went to Stockton for
the summer before my junior year. I was glad I
was going to stay with Jim and June for the summer. If anyone ever found out about the way I
felt, my mom and dad and whole family would dis-

51

own me. I just had to forget everything.

I was sixteen and June said I was a woman and should start acting like it. She cut my hair in bangs and she painted my finger nails and gave me two sheath dresses. June took me to work and introduced me to everyone. I met this girl with the same name as mine and she and I became friends. She had dark hair and wore real sexy clothes and was very pretty. June and her mom were best friends. June started calling me Sherry, she said she liked that name better and also when Sharon Crain and I were always together it was better for her to call me Sherry.

At work we delivered trays to the hospital rooms. I was walking down the hall and this woman ask me if I could speak English.

"Sure, I can speak English."

"My dear your so blond that I thought you must have just come to this country from Sweaden."

Wow, I wonder if that was a burn? (burn ment cut low or remark)

Oh well, I started handing out trays. There was this nun in one of the rooms and she was the sweetest person and always smiled, she was dieing from cancer. It was a catholic hospital and my dad did not think much of catholics but he let me work there after begging him a whole month.

This one day I really felt cheerful and got a tray and walked into this room. I almost droped the tray, this old man was lieing there uncovered and had this catheter connected and I thought I was going to faint. I put the tray down real fast and ran out of the room. I was shaking all over and I had to lean against the hall wall because I felt so sick and was about to faint.

I was sure glad when they put me washing dishes. At first scraping thoes plates made me sick but I just kept on and pretty soon it didn't bother me. I also got to work in the fountain for a week while this girl was on vacation.

I came home from work and June ask me if I would like a glass of beer. June said, she would

rather have her kid drink beer in front of her
than behind her back and I was sixteen and a
glass or two of beer wouldn't hurt me. Well,
when I got to the second glass of beer I was so
dizzy I had to go lay down. The walls were spin-
ning and everything was going around, it was the
worst feeling I ever had. Finally I put my foot
out on the floor and that helped.

On friday or saterday night Jim and June would
take me to this beer bar and I would drink coke
and they would drink beer. The name of the place
was Chris and Inks, and this man and woman owned
it. There was this big guy, Tiney, he would come
in there and they had a special chair for him at
the end of the bar. Tiney weighted about 300 lbs.
Everybody use to joke and talk and it was a lot
of fun.

This one night we stopped into Chris and Inkies, and Tiney and Chris was having a argument.

"Tiney you would not have enough guts to meet
me at 9:00 O'clock down at one of those skid row
bars."

"Look, lady you don't have enough guts and
I'll bet you ten bucks. So put your money where
your mouth is."

At a quarter to nine Tiney got up and said,
"Who wants to go with me to meet Chris at that
skid row bar, but I bet she won't even show."

Tiney talked Jim and June into going and all
the way down there they kept telling me to keep
the door locked and not to open it to anyone
while they went in there. We got there and I sat
in the car. Jim and June got out and then Tiney
said, "Tell her to come on."

"She's not twentyone."

"Oh hell, tell her to latch on to Roy."

This man came over and put his arm through
mine and smiled. He was handsome and seemed real
nice. The bar was dirty and these poor people
were sitting there. Most of them were drunk and
this old woman sat there with all this make up
on her face and was laughing real loud and did

53

not seem happy.

Roy, ordered me a seven up and got a drink with a shot of whiskey on the side, then he put the whiskey in my seven up and winked at me. Chris came in and everyone laughed. Roy got me another drink and I felt real funny. Then we went to this other bar and when he got me the third drink I knew I was drunk. He ask me to dance and held me real close. He ask me if I would like to go to the show with him. After the dance I ask June if I could go to the show with him.

"Sherry, he's thirty two, he's older than your brother."

We left the bar and I was really sick. We went into the house and I did not make it to the bathroom. I vomited all over everywhere. I was so sick. Jim was so mad at me, I vomited all over their rug and everything. Jim said he did not know I was drinking. "If mom and dad find out about this June and I will be on there shit list."

"I'm not going to tell them, I won't tell anyone, I'm sorry."

Sue, Bob's wife, was going to have a baby. Bob was just starting a new job and they didn't have very much and I could tell they were worried. My brother treated Sue so mean. He didn't have to do that.

One night we were in Chris and Inkies and Bob came in. He had on this torn shirt and he smiled. It was Jims birthday. Bobs birthday was just a couple of days from Jims. Everyone sang happy birthday to Jim. Bob got a plate of food and acted like he was really hungry.

"If the pigs leave anything, the rest of us will have something."

I felt like sluging that guy that said that in the face. Him saying that and my brother sitting there like a hungry little kid in his torn shirt. They could take there food and shove it up there ass. He really smiled when I gave him, his present. Bob said he had to go home and when he left that same s.o.b. said, "Just eat and run!"

I had a rotten time the rest of the night.
People sure could be mean.

Tiney came over to Jim and Junes a couple of
weeks later and we were all drinking beer and Tiney was really upset. Him and this woman were having an affair and she was going to leave her
husband and they went to Reno, so she could get
a divorce. She changed her mind when her husband
came after her.

"Jim I want to barrow your gun."

"What do you want my gun for?"

"Never mind, just give me your god dam gun!"

"I'm not going to give you my gun!"

"I want'a go over there and blow both there
god dam heads off."

"Tiney, I know what it's like to love someone
that don't love you, it really hurts."

"What's a kid like you know?"

"I'm not very old but I really do understand."

"Thanks kid."

Tiney sat there and tears was rolling down
his checks. I felt so sorry for him.

"You know I got a neice, and you remind me of
her. She got killed on her graduation night a
year ago. Oh shit lets have a party and forget
all this bull shit."

Tiney was a truck driver and he could get
some hot beef for half price so Jim and June
gave him some money. He skiped town with there
money. I couldn't hate him, even after he did
that.

June and I were talking about friends and I
told her about my dad saying there was no such
thing as a friend. He said he did not want any
dam friends. "Sherry, I'll tell you one thing
there is no two women that can be friends. Wom-
en, or females can't get along. You can't trust
a female, when Jim and I first got married he
was running around with this female, about four
months after we were married. I took care of her,
but I'll never forgive him for that."

"If you love him you can forgive him can't

you?"

"There are things you can't forget Sherry."

"I thought you guys had a perfect marriage."

"No one has a perfect marriage."

"If you and Jim ever split up it would really hurt me."

"I'm not planning on it but if we do, we do."

"I really love you guys."

"Sherry, I don't want you to tell anyone this, but you are our favorite. I know how your mom and dad favor Kerry. They use to favor Bob over Jim too. Sherry, I want to tell you something else, you ought to quit having anything to do with that Janice. I told your mom a long time ago to keep you away from her."

Wow, if they knew the way I felt about Jan and the way I always felt deep down inside, they would all disown me. They always blamed Jan for everything.

Sharon Crain and I were going to the Stockton state fair. We got a bus to the fair grounds and started walking around, where all the rides and games were. We rode on the hammar and Sharon was scared and my stomach felt like it was in my throat, when we went up and around and then when we stopped at the top, we could see the whole city but I felt suspended and when I looked at the ground it scared me. We rode on a lot of rides but the one I disliked the most was the faris wheel. Sharon thought it was really funny because I was scared on the faris wheel, she thought it was really fun.

It was getting late so we walked to the nearest bus stop and waited for the bus. Sharon was going to spend the night with me. This tall black man walked up to the bus stop and he had a bag of grocerys in his arms. He ask Sharon about the buses and I was thinking about Jim and June being mad at me for being so late. We had spent all our money except for our bus fair, so when Sharon ask me, "Sherry, come on let's get a coke."

"We don't have any money for cokes."

"Come on, lets get a coke."

"Whats amatter with you?"

Sharon grabed me by the arm and started walking real fast. "He's after us come on."

I looked back and the man was comming towards us. Then I was so scared I was running and passed Sharon. We ran about two blocks and he was catching up to us when we ran across the street and a car pulled up in front of us.

"Hey, where you going in such a hurry?"

It was two boys and Sharon went up to their car and said, "A man is chasing us."

The man saw the car and he started running down a side street. The two boys told us to get in the car and we would see where the man went. The man disapeared and then we decided we should go to the police because Sharon said, he exposed himself to her.

We went to the police station and we gave our names and Sharon told them what happened. They said they would put out a A.P.B. with his description. We left the police station and the boys ask us if we wanted to go and have a cup of coffee.

"That nigger ought to be caught and shot!"

I did not like the word nigger and I knew it was awful what that man did but I did not like the word nigger.

We drank some coffee and then the boys ask us if we wanted to go riding around. Sharon said, she did not want to go to Jim and Junes because she was so upset, so we went to this park by the Stockton harbor. We went down to the water and went wading in the water. It was sure silly but thats what Sharon wanted to do. Then the boys took us to Jim and Junes and let us out of the car about a block away.

We walked up to the house and opened the door and Jim was standing talking on the phone and did not have any clothes on. When he saw us he put the phone down and ran in the bedroom. June

was really mad and ask us where had we been, because the police had called and told them what
happened and wanted us to come to the police station to identify the man that chased us. Sharon
said, that we had walked home and thats why it
took us so long.

Jim took us to the police station and we had
to give a statement and then they took us behind
this one way mirror and ask us to identify this
man. Sharon said, he was the one. I told them I
did not know because I did not look that close
at him. The police said the man did not have a
bag of grocerys but a bag of sex books.

Jim and June said me staying there with them
that summer had caused them to have grey hair
and they were glad they did not have any teen a-
gers. Jim was worried about what happened, mess-
ing up his chances on becomming a policeman.
Well, it did not mess him up and the next month
Jim would be a policeman.

Sue had twins, a boy and a girl. The little
boy died. June and I had stopped at Chris and
Inkes when Bob came in and told us. This guy
came up and ask Bob if his wife had her baby yet.

"Ya, she had a girl."

"Whats a matter weren't you man enough to
have a boy?"

Bob did not say anything. If they only new
they wouldn't think that!

My mom and dad were suppose to come to take
me home on a friday and they never came. Janice
had planned a surprise party for me but I was
the only one that never got there for it. Everyone said, my surprise party was really fun. I
felt so bad.

I was home about a week, when Janice and Hel-
en said, I had changed and I acted like I was
better than anyone else. They said, they wished
I would act like I use to. Wow, it seemed I could
not do anything right. They said, I talked and
acted like a white shoe and even looked like one
with my hair in bangs and my painted finger nails.

58

"Your a goodie, goodie!"
"I'm no dam goodie, goodie! I'm me!"

Chapter Eight

It was nice being back home. I was going to start my junior year and with four lambs wool sweaters that I bought with my money. With the money from my Income Tax return, I could buy my class ring. I quit talking nice and everyone wasn't mad at me any more.
I didn't think I was better than anyone else, and I was glad they weren't mad any more.

We started having parties on the weekends. There were always one or more of our parents there and we use to play this game called kiss, slap, or hug. One person sat in a chair and someone stood behind them and held their eyes and said, who do you want to do this to and made a sign of a kiss, slap, or hug. The person in the chair would give a name for each sign and then would have to kiss, slap, or hug three people of the opposite sex. That game was our favorite and was the most fun. On Christmas we decided to give each other gag gifts because none of us had any money. My sister gave Allen a box of exlax and a roll of toilet paper; he got mad and fed the exlax to all the dogs in the neighborhood. Ray gave Betty a baby bottle and a box of tooth picks, the thought being she was thin and childish, or more to the point, just to make her mad. Well at that party mostly everyone got good and mad. I got a lemon that had written on it, to make you sweeter.

One day someone thought up the idea of collecting cow manure in paper sacks and at night we went around to different houses and set the bags on door steps, lit them on fire and then knocked on the door. Well, when the people saw the fire they stomped it out and got a shoe full of cow

manure. We laughed and laughed until we got
caught and it was explained to us how dangerous
that could be, so we didn't do it any more.

One day at school a gang of white shoe boys
surrounded Helen, she just stood there scared to
death while they held her in a circle making dirty remarks to her.

"Hey, baby are you any good?"

"How many guys you had sweetie?"

I wanted to throw up, but all we could do was
take it because who was going to stand up against
half the foot ball team? Then on the way home
some punk said all of us girls were whores and I
was the biggest whore of all. Wow was I mad, I
had about had it and the kids had to stop me because I was going to break that kids neck. They
laughed and thought it was really funny about me
being such a big whore.

The lady that lived across the street from Helen was always talking about us and saying we
were really awful. One day Helen was walking home
with her boy friend Bobby and he kissed her and
that lady saw it and said, "Helen Norton, nice
girls don't do that."

"Why don't you mind your own business."

"Well, your mother will hear about this."

Helen got put on restriction for a week for
talking back to a older person disrespectfully.
We all got together and decided that we were going to get even with that old bag. What would be
the meanest thing we could think of to do to her.
I don't know who thought of it but we got a kotex pad and put catsup and vinager and mustard on
it and wrote this note, ride this out of town
and Janice volunteered to sneek over and tack it
on her door. We turned all the lights off in the
house and stood by the window to watch Jan do it.
Jan sneeked up to the door and tacked it on the
door and knocked real loud on the door. She started to run and sliped in some mud, and the ladies husband almost grabed her by her sweat shirt.
She started running down the street and got away

and we were all laughing and trying to be quiet. Well the lady called the police and said this ruff gang was out to take her life and had threaten her and told her to get out of town. Helen's dad knew it was us so he called this meeting and gave this talk about what a awful thing we did and Helen was going to get two more weeks added to her restriction. He ask us if we were sorry and told us we all ought to get into trouble for scaring that lady. Jan got up and started to walk out and said, "I'm not sorry, I wouldn't of done it if I was going to be sorry."

It was friday night and all the boys were going out together and all us girls were going out together. Betty got her dads car and we went to the drive in. This car parked beside us with three sailors. They kept flirting with us and started talking to us. Well, Jan said, we would meet them at the store. tomarrow. She gave them directions to the store by where we lived. So the next day we went to the store and talked to them and the next weekend we were going out with them. My dad would have a fit and I was not going to ask him. Jan said, I could spend the night at her house and then my parents wouldn't know. Jan sure was sexy the way she flirted with thoes guys and she was sure pretty.

Joan was going to go with us on the date and she was a nut. She thought Jan and I were gods, and would stand and look at me and Jan with this weird look and say, you guys are wonderful. She said, some of the crazyest things and told some of the sillyest stories. She said, her ten year old sister still craped her pants and this one day her sister was sitting on this lumber pile craping her pants and Joan ask her what she was doing.

"Sally, what are you doing?"
"Nothing."
"What's your face so red for?"
"I'm thinkin."
"Your craping your pants aren't you?"

"No! I'm just thinkin I told you."

I couldn't help but laugh and Joan was always doing some of the crazyest things. She liked this boy and when she found out it was a lost cause she went on a hunger strick. Then there was the time she heard that the world was comming to an end, so she ate 10 boxes of candy that she was suppose to sell and did not do her home work. That day I went over her house and she was in her bedroom praying and I came in and one of those air rade wornings came on the radio and she jumped up and grabed me and I thought she was going to chock me to death before I got it across to her that the world wasn't comming to an end. She said, just wait and it will, but it didn't so then she started on something else.

"Sharon, your so grown up and so worldly."

"Quit saying that stuff, will ya."

"Well, I just wanted to say on this date I am going to really act grown up and worldly."

"I don't even think I want to go."

"I guess your use to dates and men."

"Oh, hell Joan!"

Well, we went on the date friday and we ended up parked out some where with a bunch of beer and made out. The guy I was with was o.k. but I didn't like the way he kissed. I wished we could have went some where instead of parking. Everytime I drank I really got sick. I spent the rest of the night with my head out the window. One good thing about drinking was that I could talk better when I drank. Joan was in love and I just hoped she would not go on another hunger strick.

I took Psychology and it was my favorite subject. It was just wonderful the way people could be helped and not locked up in rooms and hid away like they use to do. I knew if my dad could go to a psychoanalyst he would probably feel a lot better but I sure could not walk up to my dad and say, hey dad why don't you go over and visit the local psychoanalyst. My mom and dad did not like psychology they said. "If someone

63

is nuts, there nuts."

"Some people have problems and psychology is one of the most wonderful things that has been discovered."

"Sharon, you don't know what lifes about. Remember that woman at the mines that escaped from Napa, they took her away in a straight jacket, and she's still locked up. If your nuts your nuts."

I just did not talk about psychology to my parents, because we just ended up in a big fight. We took this test at school and it said I was a intravert, extravert and I was self centered. Wow, self centered means all you think about is yourself. It means I'm selfish. Wow I think the worst thing in the world is to be selfish, and I'm selfish. I ask Jan if she thought I was selfish? "No your not selfish, why?"

"Nothing I was just wondering."

"Whats a matter with you anyway?"

"Nothing."

Jan and Joan spent the night sleeping out in my back yard. When my mom and dad went to bed we sneeked out and went walking around. Jan broke her bra and then she said, "I've really got a neat idea, lets hang this bra on the street sign by the bachelors house o.k?"

So thats what we did and almost did not make it back home because we were laughing so hard.

One night I was walking Jan home and she said, "Lets rob some glove compartments."

I said, "O.k."

We found some car doors open then we robed the glove compartments and took gear shift knobs and flatened some tires. I don't know why but I felt good, and this feeling came over me and I felt better around everything and I wasn't scared. The next day I really felt bad and I was scared. Wow, I sure did not want to go to the juve.

My mom and dad would go away for the weekend to visit Jim and Bob and would let Kerry and I stay home. Kerry was really something I had to promise her my life to get her to do anything

and couldn't leave her alone. Jan and Joan and I
decided to rob this house next door to Joan's because the people were gone on vacation. So we
got Kerry to go visit her friend and then we went
over there and I got the window open then we went
inside and took some stuff. Then we got the lady
next door to my house to buy us a bottle, we saved our lunch money all week. Kerry came back
and called us a bunch of no good drunks. Then
Joan drank two glasses of straight vodka and got
up and tryed to walk a make believe line. She
was really a nut. Then I was sick and went in
the bathroom and turned the water on my head. I
spent the whole night in the bathroom vomiting
and running cold water on my head.

About a week later my mom said, the cops were
looking for some robbers and she hoped they
found them. I told Jan and Joan and we were really scared.

"Well, I won't be around to go to jail because my dad will kill me," Joan said, as she
walked back and forth across her bedroom floor.

"Look they don't know it was us."

"Jan, my mom acted like she knew and she
would tell on us."

"Look, let's not worry till we know something."

"I wish the world would have come to an end
when it was suppose to have."

My dad was really getting mean I came back
from Joan's after dark and he slaped me and knocked me down and kicked me in the side, then my
mom pulled him off me. He said, he did not even
like me running around with that god dam prota-
gee Jan and I was suppose to be in the house before dark. He said, he ought to put me in the juve. Wow if he knew about that house, I'd probably spend the rest of my life in prison.

The kids at school were knocking themselves
out. You bent over and took ten deep breaths and
then stood up and blew on your thomb. Jan, Joan
and I were on the lawn at my house doing it and
laughing at the funny way we acted. Joan would

just lay there and jump and jerk and Jan looked
like she was sucking her thumb and I would always jump up and start running. My mom decided
we were nuts and she didn't know what to do about it.

We decided to steal some of our parents liquor and get drunk on this one saterday after
noon. My dad drank his wine so fast I could not
get any but Jan and Joan got enough to get us
high. We were sitting there and Joan had this
red bulb and these red curtains, in her bedroom
and the room was this pretty red color and I
felt warm and nice from the liquor.

"Hey, Sharon how do you make out?"

"I don't know, why?"

"I just wonder how you and Jan make out, why
don't we just see there isn't nothing wrong with
that."

"I don't know."

I don't know why but I was scared and my
blood started rushing all through my body and my
voice sounded funny.

"I'll kiss Jan first."

Joan kissed Jan and then she told me too. I

kissed Jan and my whole body was acting funny
and I wished the soft sweetness of her kiss
could last forever. I was shaking so bad I could
not hold my glass of whiskey. Joan came over and
kissed me and then I felt like a bomb was inside
of me and it was going to go off any minute.
Joan smelled real nice and she kissed almost as
good as Jan. I never felt like that before in my
life and I just sat there and did not feel like
I was even there. Then I walked Jan home and she
never said anything and wow maybe she did not
feel the way I did. Then I went back to Joans
and we started talking and then we started making out and her body was close to mine and her
soft mouth, oh I told her we better stop because
my body was shaking so bad it scared me. I went
home and I could not stop thinking about Jan and
Joan. Wow, Jan acted like it wasn't anything.
Wow, and Reatha thought she was the queer. Oh, I
didn't know what to do, oh, wow, if anyone knew
how I felt.

My sister Billie was going to vist us for a
couple of weeks. She and her husband lived in
West Virginia and she and her little boy were
flying to Calif. We went to the air port in Oakland to meet her. She got off that plain with
her little boy and it was the saddest thing I e-
ver saw she was pregnant and tears were running
down her checks and she looked like a poor lost
person. She put her arms around mom and dad and
really started crying. Her little boy stood
there in a little suit with this scared look on
his face. Jamie, was 14 months old and that was
the first time we had ever seen him. He was named after my dad and brother Jim.

Billie had been staying with us for a week
when she got this letter from her next door
neighbor. Chester, her husband had disappeared.
The front door had been left open and the fan
was on and all his clothes were there but he was
gone. Billie started screaming and crying and
crying and acted like she was going to lose her

mind or her baby, she was carrying. Jamie was
crying and screaming too. My mom went over to
her and said, "Shut up, shut up, your going to
scare Jamie to death."

Billie called Chester's mother and every
where else but he had just disapeared. There Billie was with a fourteen month old little kid and
one on the way and my dad did not make enough money to take care of all of us. The county said
they could not help Billie because she had not
been in the state long enough to get aid.

"I told you that Red assed bastard wasn't no
god dam good didn't I?"

"Ya dad."

Billie was so upset, she cryed and cryed and
Jamie screamed and my mom and dad didn't know
what they were going to do. My sister Kerry helped
Billie with Jamie, and acted real grown up about
everything. My aunt came to see us and she said
she could help Billie get on welfare in the county where she lived and her and my mom sat down
with Billie and figured out a story to tell them.
Billie said, she was scared and was afraid that
she would get caught and put in jail and have
her kids taken away from her. Billie did not
have a choice tho because we just did not have
enough money to support all of us.

I'll never forget the day we took Billie to
Ukiah. She was so scared and Kerry was going to
go with her and stay to help her when the baby
came. Kerry would go to school there. Billie and
Kerry were going to stay with this woman until
Billie could get a place. My aunt had everything
fixed up so Billie could get on welfare and my
mom and dad would send her some money too. When
we left them there, Billie and Kerry were crying
and I felt sick. Billie looked so sad all pregnant and everything. My mom never cryed but her
voice shook and the wrinkels in her face showed
more and her hair was greying. When my mom looked like that I hurt so bad inside.

Chapter Nine

I was going on a feild
trip with my psychology
class, to the Napa State
hospital. The teacher
told us that this was a
serious feild trip and
none of us were suppose
to be funny. On the way
there in the bus one of
the kids told this joke.
This man was giving a
lecture to the patients

in a state hospital and he began by saying, "Do
you all know why your here?" One of the patients
stood up and said, "Because we're not all there."
    When we got there, we were taken to this room
where we were suppose to sit in on the patients
meeting. The doctor said, they had meetings to
descuss the problems they had and to give them a
common goal, or something like that. Any way
these five people came in and had a meeting about this woman that did her laundry every morning at 4:00 a.m. Some of the kids laughed, but I
really felt sorry for those people. I thought it
was awful them sitting there so serious and trying to descuss something that was important to
them and a room full of kids, that I think did
not really understand and were trying to keep
from laughing. The patients left and then the
doctor told us what was wrong with them. This
little old lady was Schizophrenic, and a lady
that looked like my sister was Manic-depressive,
she made me feel so sad, I wanted to cry when I
looked at her.
    Then they took us through the wards and I
felt sick all over. This one ward had all these
poor people sitting there and they were all de-
formed and there arms and legs looked like rub-
ber. I was glad when we left and started walking
to this park on the grounds. Then we passed this

69

separate building that the teenagers were in.
When they saw us they yelled and hung on to the
bars of the window and begged us to give them a
cigarette or to come up to the window and talk
to them. I wished I'd never come on that dam
trip, I felt so sad and depressed over the whole
thing.

All the kids ask me how I liked going to Napa,
and did I see any nuts. I told them I didn't
want to talk about it. They ask me what was a
matter with me, didn't I have a sence of humor?

It was me and my mom's birthday. I was born
on my mom's birthday. I was seventeen and she
was fifty two. I saved my money and bought her a
rose tree. She loved roses and she wanted a rose
tree very much. I told my mom and dad I did not
want a present but if all us kids put our money
together and bought everything, would they let
me have a water skiing party down at the river.
They said yes and I could not believe it. All
the kids bought hot dogs and made salads and we
got two other cars to take us to the river.

There was about twenty of us and I started
helping everyone learn to water ski. Leo got up
the first time, but skied all bent over and I
thought my mom was going to die laughing, as she
watched. Jan could ski very well and she had on
this real sexy bathing suit and the boys were
following her around. Then it was Joans turn to
ski. First Joan had to wave at everyone, then I
thought she was going to drown me before I could
get the skis on her. I wasn't going to lose my
temper. In teaching you must remain calm.

"Joan, do you want to learn how to ski?"

"What do you think I'm sitting in this cold
water for?"

"Now remember to keep bent down and hang on,
okay? Now when you are ready yell at my dad."

The next moments were more than unbelievable.
First she started off with a mighty "Let her go
Daddy O!" Then she was up, no she was down, no
she was to the side. Two skis were up in the air,
70

but where was Joan? Oh no, she was still hanging
on to the rope and my dad didn't know it. All
you could see was the top of her head skimming a-
cross the water and the fool wouldn't let go.

As they pulled up to the shore I looked at
Joan's face and it looked like a dried prune.
Boy, was she mad. "You tried to kill me!" She
yelled. "You told me to hang on to the rope so I
did and I almost drowned."

Everyone laughed and Joan started walking up
and down the beach kicking sand all over and
then everyone jumped up and started a big sand
fight. My mom started yelling that we were getting sand in the food and sure enough we ended
up eating sandy everything.

Everyone thought that was the best party we
ever had. I really felt good and my mom and dad
had a good time and liked all the kids. My mom
just got mad because my dad got drunk.

Jan, Joan and I were going out with the sailors again. Neil the guy I was always with had a
very nice custom car and I guess he was my boy
friend. I just up and took him to my house and
introduced him to my mom and dad. They did not
say anything, I was really surprised. We told
the guys we wanted to go some where because we
were tired of just parking and drinking beer.
They did not like it but they took us to San Fransisco to play land. Then on the way home we got
some beer and they started talking about how
they got money when they were broke. They said,
that one of them would get out on the highway
and the other would park the car and watch.
Then the one walking would act real nelly and
try to get picked up by a queer. Well if a queer
picked the one walking up, the other would follow and then they would get the guy in his apartment and roll him. What could the guy do, go to
the police and tell them he picked up a guy and
then got rolled. Then everyone started saying
how they hated queers and how we ought to just
ride around and find one and beat them up. I did-

n't say anything but I was sure glad they did not know about me. The thing that really hurt was hearing Jan say those things. Wow everyone sure was wrong about her.

Jan's mom worked for the county as a typist and she knew these women at work that were starting a softball team. Jan's mom was the nicest person I knew and she said I was her third daughtor. She did everything for Jan and was such a lady. She invited some of the women over to meet Jan and I. They were really great. They laughed and kided and this one was talking about the others boy friend. "Your boy friend is really cute eccept for the dent in his head, but for 300 lbs, he's tall, 5 ft. 1."

We laughed and talked about softball and they wanted us to try out for the team. If we made the team we would travel all over California and get our pictures in the paper. Those women were really wonderful. They had good jobs and some of them were married but they were all very good ball players and they wanted us to try out for there team. The wanders was a team in a California womens softball league.

We tryed out for the team and made it. Jan was second base and they said I could play center feild. Playing center feild was a honor because you had to be fast and cover a lot of ground and they thought I was really a good batter. My mom and dad did not want to let me play ball because they were afraid I would get hurt. Wow, but I begged and pleaded and finally they let me play but every time I left they would go on and on about how I was going to get a broken leg.

Pat and Donna used to come and pick Jan and I up and I could never even talk to them, they were so great, I was afraid to talk to them. Jan always did most of the talking anyway. Donna said, I was the most backward person she ever met and they ask Jan if I could talk. I didn't like that but I just couldn't talk around them,

72

I was even worst than I was at school.

The first game came and when I got out on the feild I never was so scared in my life. All those people looking at me, I was even afraid to move. I prayed the ball won't come to me because I was so scared. Everyone ask me what was wrong but I couldn't explain, or tell them how I felt. Everyone was really disapointed in me and could not figure out how I could be so good at practice and mess up like I did. I got better and was hitting good, but I was not doing as good as I could because I was afraid of the people looking at me and yelling. Jan and I had our names in the paper and our pictures and when I hit two home runs everyone called me babe ruth. I was embarassed. I really wanted to play ball and all the women were so great but I really didn't like a lot of attention.

At school I set a new record for the softball throw and Jan and I got our letter sweaters. I think it was about the proudest moment of our lives. The girls that got there letter sweaters were usually white shoes. We were seniors and had other privileges too. Jan was named editor of the senior edition, a booklet that told different things about all the seniors. Jan put a lot of things in the senior edition about the black shoes and everyone else. It was about the first year that the senior edition wasn't all white shoe. Janice was voted funniest girl in the senior class and I was voted shyest.

Then came the biggest day of all, we had been in the badmitten play offs for two weeks and this final match would be it. We had dreamed of winning the badmitten trophy for four years and now, this was it. The two girls we were to play were really good.

"Sharon were going to win, we are, we really are."

"I don't know."

"Remember we're going to win."

We started playing and it was the best and

73

closest game the gym teacher said, she ever saw
and with the last point being called wood, we really won. Everyone there jumped up and ran over
to us and we were going to the Clarmont hotel in
Berkeley to eccept our trophy at a big banquet.
Wow that scared me. I'll never forget that big
banquet and that big fancy place. My mom had to
buy my graduation dress early so I could wear it.
I had to wear high heels, I couldn't walk in.
They had this buffet or al-a-cart or something
and they served snails and squid and Janice was
eating it. She made me take some but I almost
vomited, "Do you want me to throw up hear in
front of everyone before we get our trophy?"

Then we had to get up in front of everyone
and exxept our trophy, and I was scared. Jan did
the talking and at the end of the speech I said
"me too". I was glad when that was over.

We were really popular at school, everyone
would say high and just walk over to talk to us.
We sat on the senior bench and the whole world
seemed different. I felt confused tho, I knew I
wasn't good but I did not want to believe I was
bad. Sometimes I wished someone could just say
Sharon your this or your that and then my mind
could just quit worrying. What if I really was
rotten to my very core. I don't want to believe
I'm bad and I think I am. So if someone would
just plain say Sharon your rotten and no good, I
couldn't face it and would just keep on being
confused. Why did everything have to be so dam
complex. Jan would get mad at me and say, "You
always make everything so complicated."

She was right, but I just couldn't understand
things. Nothing was positive, I did not understand. There's so many sides to everything. Everyone seems to see things so clear. At home my
dad never kept his mouth shut. He kept yelling
and I couldn't move without him telling me, lift
your cigarette 10 degrees to the left and now 10
degrees to the right. Wow, I could hardly breathe.
My dad made me feel like I was locked in a room

and the walls were slowly going to crush me to
death. I wanted to leave home so bad. I wanted
to leave ever sence I can remember. I was frightened. What was I going to do? I couldn't go to
college after graduation and that was what I wanted more than anything. My parents couldn't afford to send me to junior college and I had to
find a job, but what could I do? If only I had
some kind of training. Boy, graduating from high
school didn't mean anything. If I knew someone
that could give me a job I'd be o.k. I couldn't
work at the hospital, June already told me that.
The kids that have parents that hire them right
after graduation sure are lucky. You have to
have experience before you get a job and you have
to have a job before you get experience. Wow, it's
really hard starting out. I didn't have a license and my father didn't want me to drive and I
didn't have a car. I was really worried and Jan
was so dam calm.
     One day at school this recruiting officer
came to school and told us about the armed for-
ces and how you could learn a skill and travel.
I could do something for my country. My brothers
fought in the wars and now even tho I was a girl
I could do my part. I could just see it, I could
do something good and even learn a trade. It was
the only way and I could send home money and
help my mom and dad.
     Kerry and I went with my mom and dad to visit
Bob and Sue. Charmaine was there and she was the
first one I told about my idea. Charmaine said
if I waited until Sept. after graduation, she
would join with me. She would be eighteen then
and I would be eighteen in may. Gerene came o-
ver and we were talking and I about fell over.
The same two girls that said they would give a
kiss as a reward at the door on there first date
had some different ideas. Charmaine said, "This
friend of ours got married and was a virgin and
she said it spoiled her weding night, it's also
better to know if you really enjoy each other be-

75

fore your married."

"Well, a, I guess so, a."

"We've talked it over and decided thats what we'll do if we find someone we really love, we wouldn't just go around doing it with everyone."

"Well, a, ya, I guess not."

Charmaine said she would talk to the recruiting officer in Stockton and we would tell them we were going to enlist together.

When I told Jan she said I was nuts and she was going to have two of the girls on the ball team talk to me. They had been in the service. She just did not understand that I really didn't have much of a choice. She wouldn't even talk about getting out of school.

"Enjoy today and hell with tomarrow."

Well, she did not have a dad like mine. She did not get along with her stepfather and he beat on her mom but she sure wasn't worrying. I'll bet she would miss me when I was gone. Her stepfather made a pass at her and her sister.

I showed my book to my English teacher. She said, I sure made a lot of grammar mistakes. I wrote my first short story. "Brilliance of the Fading Sun." It was about my dog smoky. Mrs. Leslie ask me to send it to the Diablo Valley Pageant of arts. She said for me not to get my hopes up, because I would be compeating with adults and college students. One judge put my story in fourth place. Mrs. Leslie said I should really be proud of that. I got an award from her for creative writing and I got this little china statue. It ment as much to me as the badmitten trophy, maybe more because I really wanted to be a writer. I wrote another short story, "The Long Winter." It was about mom, dad, Billie, Jim, and Bob. I was going to keep on writing even if everyone thought I was crazy.

Chapter Ten

Janice and I walked ov-
er to her house after
school. There was a
short cut to her house
and the road was called
the dump road. The two
houseing tracks we liv-
ed in were right next
to each other. Behind a
hill was the city dump.
The dump road ran along
side of the tracks. The
dump trucks had to drive through the houseing
tracks to get to the dump road. People didn't
like that because the trucks had come close to
running over kids a couple of times. On windy
days when they burned at the dump it really smelled bad too. The people tryed to get them to
stop burning but it didn't do any good. We got
to Jans house and started talking. When Jan got
a big smile on her face, I knew she thought of
something.

"Sharon, would you like a martini?"

"What do they taste like?"

"I'll fix one and you can see. I can really
make a good martini, I mak'em all the time for
my mom."

We went in Jan's den. It was really nice.
Jan's dad had built a bar, and her mom had all
these funny signs on the wall.

"<u>Once a king always a king, but once a nights
enough</u>."

"<u>Everything I like is either immoral, illegal,
or fattning</u>."

"Here ya go, I even got a olive and a lemon
peal in your first martini. Well how do you like
it?"

I took a drink and I thought I was going to
chock, my throat was on fire.

"Jan, it's awful."

"Well, it tastes like it's just boose and no mix."

"Stupid, thats what it is. You should see my aunt pack them away. You would think she was drinking coke."

I was really disappointed when I tasted the martini. It was really awful, and in the movies someone was always drinking martinis. "What are you two up to?"

We turned around and there stood Jan's mom, with her hands on her hips and this descusted look on her face. I thought Jan's mom looked like Jane Russel, eccept she was small and didn't have big chests and her hair was cut short and was grey. I guess I should say her face looked like Jane Russels face. Any way she sure was mad.

"So that's where my liquor has been disappearing to. What's the meaning of this Janice Mitchal?"

"Sharon never had a martini before."

"Well Miss Mitchal, I have a fabulous idea, you two can just spend the evening here tonight and I will furnish you with all you can drink. We'll just see if we can dry up your thurst, but it will be a case of beer that will have to do the trick. Not my liquor in the bar I keep for my guests. Call your mother Sharon and ask if you can spend the night. No, I'll call her."

Jan's mom went to call my mom and I was worried because I didn't know what she would say. I knew she wouldn't tell on me but my mom and dad didn't like Jan and could really be snotie. My mom said some mean things about Jan's mom, and it really hurt me because I thought Marty was just about the greatest person I knew.

"Sharon, your spending the night. I'll go to the store and then we'll sit down and have some drinks and talk. The three of us haven't had a talk in a long time."

Marty, was very intelligent and spoke nicely. She also had the best sence of humor and always kidded me. When Jan and I got in a fight she always stuck up for me and told Jan I was the best friend she ever had and that she didn't appreciate me. Marty use to put her arm around me and tell me she loved me and that I was her third daughtor. I really loved her too. My mom use to really get mad at me when I talked about Marty. I loved my mom but I loved Marty too.

We drank beer and talked and was really having a good time. Jan and I told Marty all about school and how everything was happening and how much fun it was being seniors. Marty told us how proud she was about the badmitten championship and the other activities we were in.

"Well, kids I'm going to retire until the marrow."

"Oh mom!"

"See you kids in the morning."

We kept on drinking and talking. I was really getting high and so was Jan. She was sitting in this chair and this song was playing on the record player. "Heavenly, heavenly, thats what you are, you are to me. A guiding light in the night so heavenly for only me. I need you oh so much, I long for your tender touch, heavenly is what you are to me."

I felt those words and even more, when I looked at Jan. She looked so sexy, her eyes deep brown and her hair hanging lose, her face so soft, and her skin so brown and lovely. I couldn't take my eyes off of her. She looked at me and then she told me to come over to her. I was shaking so much and I felt hot all over and I couldn't breath. I knelt by her chair and looked into her eyes and then she kissed me. She run her hands through my hair, and I pulled her close to me. I felt her body next to mine, and all her softness. Her lips were wet from drinking and she moved her lips on mine with soft gentelness, and the touch sent wild chills through my whole body. My body was throbing and my heart beating, oh Jan I love you. Then she pulled away,

"We have to stop."

I didn't want to stop, I loved her.

"Sharon, my mom, she might find out."

I got up and went over and sat down in the other chair and took a drink of beer.

"We drank to much, we're not like that, I couldn't ever be like that because it would kill my mom."

"I'm sorry Jan."

"Let's just forget it and go to bed o.k.?"

We went to bed and I layed next to Jan, feeling her warm body next to mine and felt the wanting. Oh I never wanted anything so bad in my life. Why did I have to feel like this. I had to get up and go in the front room and have a cigarette and another beer. Wow, it was a good thing I was leaving. I could go away and everyone would be better off. I would find out that these feelings I felt were just in my head.

Neil called me and said he had a friend that wanted to go out with Jan. So we made a date for friday night, Jan said she thought blind dates were exciting and she just hoped he wasn't a lemon. I told her I ask Neil if he was a mess and he said he was a nice guy and as much as he knew about it he was nice looking. We were going to the drive in. On the way to the drive in this guy in this sharp 57 ford, all customed, pulled up next to us and wanted to drag. We followed the guy to this long stretch of road out side of town. There was a curve at the end of the straight part of the road and if a car came while they were draging there would be a hard crack up for sure.

"Someone is going to have to flag us to start. Sharon get between our cars and start the race."

"What do I do Neil?"

"Hold your hands up in the air and when you bring them down we'll start."

I stood there and both the cars revved their engines, when my hands came down, the two cars took off with screeching tires and roaring mo-

80

tors, swerving and gaining speed. We watched the corner ahead not knowing whether a car would come or not. Neil won and they slamed on their brakes and then turned around and came back.

We got to the drive in and drank some beer and then started making out. I couldn't stop thinking about Jan in the back seat making out with someone else. I felt so dam confused.

"Sharon come with me to the bathroom."

"What do you want her to come with you to the bathroom for, can't you do it on your own?"

"Neil, we want to talk girl talk."

"Oh."

We got to the bathroom and she told me the guy she was with was trying to make her and had unzipped her pants and everything. I told her I was going to tell Neil and have him take us home. She said she could handle the guy and for me not to worry. I told her just to call for me and I would knock the shit out of him.

"Sharon your so emotional, just forget what I told you."

We got back to the car and Neil said we were leaving. They wanted to get some more beer and then show us this parking place with a view. We went up on this hill and parked. Janice and the guy was really making out, and Neil was really getting fresh. They were laying down in the back seat and Neil wispered. "Let's do it too." I couldn't take it I had to get out of that car. I pushed Neil away and got out of the car. "What's wrong with you?"

I walked away from the car and stood looking at a view, I couldn't see. I felt like crying and screaming at the same time. Neil ask me what was wrong. I started crying and he tryed to put his arms around me, I ask him please leave me a-lone.

"What did I do?"

"Neil I'm sorry, I guess I drank to much."

Neil put his arm around me and we stood there. I didn't want to go back to the car. I felt like

81

I was dead and yet I was standing there. On the
way home I did not say anything, I just felt so
dead.

The next day Jan called me and said she had
to talk to me. I went over to her house and we
went for a walk. She said she didn't want me to
think she was bad I told her I didn't think that.

"Sharon, he felt me up and I just didn't stop
him. You know that he wanted me to hold him you
know where, and I did. He didn't screw me, do
you believe me?"

"I believe you."

"Sharon do you think I'm awful bad?"

"I told you I don't think your bad, it just
happened."

"You really are understanding and we'll just
forget it o.k.?"

"Sure Jan."

I went home but I couldn't stop feeling dead
inside. I didn't understand the way I felt and I
couldn't make it go away.

At school everything was happening. We had to
have senior announcements, senior pictures, rent
our cap and gown, year book, it was awful and I
hated asking my mom for money. I couldn't enjoy
any of it, all I could think of was how bad I
felt when I had to ask my mom for all that money.
There was a meeting of all the girls in G.A.A.
and everyone brought casseroles and food and we
were really having a good time. All the girls
begged Jan, Joan, Helen, Betty and I to sing
these songs we use to sing at lunch hour around
the school.

"Come on sing those songs you guys sing,
there really funny."

Jan said o.k. and we started singing.

"Sweet rosie O'Grady was a blacksmiths daughter by birth, but Rosie got tired of living and
decided to leave the earth, so Rosie swallowed a
tape measure but dieing by inches was hard, very
hard, so Rosie went out in the alley, and there
she died by the yard, poor old Rosie, da,da, da,

da, and there she died by the yard."

"Come on you guys, sing another one."

"Sing the garbage man's daughtor."

"I'm in love with the garbage man's daughtor who lives down by the swill, how sweet is the smell of the garbage her breath is sweeter still, each night as we roam through the garbage her greasy hand in mine, her clammey lips on the back of my neck, oh isn't love devine."

About then the teacher stood up and tryed to make the room come to order but it wasn't very easy and she didn't look like she thought the song was very funny but everyone else couldn't stop laughing.

My sister Billie had a baby boy and she named him Mike. The social worker she had, came over one day after she got out of the hospital and started asking her a bunch of questions and she was really scared. She didn't like telling lies and wasn't very good at it. The social worker made Billie appear before the judge and was trying to have her put in jail. There wasn't enough evidence so the judge couldn't do anything. Then the social worker tried to get Billie to give up Mike. Two of my aunts also wanted to adopt Mike. Everyone talked to Billie and told her how Mike would have a good home and she would be better off with just Jamie to take care of.

"This is my baby how can anyone ask me to give away my own baby?"

"He will be better off Billie."

My little sister Kerry was about the only one on Billies side. "Billie you don't have to do nothing, you keep your baby."

Janice told the girls on the softball team about me wanting to join the army. So they all started talking to me and telling me the bad and good points about the service. I had already made up my mind because it was the only thing I could do. I took the test and I passed it. I had to have three character references so I gave three of my teachers names.

83

Billie

I had to go for my physical and I was scared.
When they gave me the pelvic examination I cryed
and the doctor said I had to go to San Francisco

to this army hospital and be examined by these
specialists because of me only having my period
once every four years.

My recruiting officer took me to San Fransisco
and she was really nice she told me not to be
scared. They took me in this room and I had to
wait for the doctors. I never been so scared in
my life and I started crying. This nurse came in
and told me to take my cloths off from the waist
down and then put me on this table, with my feet
in these things. I was really crying and I could-
n't stop. Then these doctors came in,

"Quit being such a big baby, we're not going
to hurt you."

They examined me and I cryed and it did hurt,
all three of them examing my pelvis.

"It didn't hurt did it?"

"Yes it did."

I really got off that table fast and started
putting on my cloths and my letter sweater.

"If you started paying more attention to boys,
than sports and comb your hair, you'll be o.k."

It was a good thing I didn't have to go
through any more of that, or I wouldn't even
join the service if I were starving to death.

Billie and my mom came to my graudation and I
was really scared. The place was full of people
and when I walked up the isle and was supose to
walk down this certain row of chairs, I walked
down the wrong row. Wow right there in front of
everyone. I had to turn around and get in the
right row, the kid behind me poked me and that's
the only reason I knew I was in the wrong row. I
was so scared, I didn't know what I was doing.
Jan didn't know whether she was going to graudate
or not until up until the last minute. She sure
smiled when she got her diploma. We stood up and
sang our school song for the last time and I
think everyone had tears in there eyes. It would
be the last time some of us would ever see each
other again. Here we come world, the class of
1960.

Chapter Eleven

I talked to Charmaine
and she said, she was
not sure if she wanted
to join the service.
She said, I better just
join without her. Char-
maine wouldn't be eigh-
teen until September
and she had to lose
twenty pounds. She lau-
ghed and said, she nev-
er even lost two pounds
so she didn't know if she could lose twenty. I
was really sorry she had changed her mind. The
closer the time came for me to go, the sorryer I
was.

Both of my brothers came over and I knew they
were going to give me a lecture. I did not mind
them telling me what they thought but they never
thought much of anything Kerry or I did.

Bob was in the Korean War and received some
metals but he never would talk about it and every time someone ask him about it he got mad. I
think he had something to do with bomb tests or
something. I think it was something secret, must
of been really secret too, because I sure could-
n't find out what it was.

Jim joined the service at the end of World
War II. He was not old enough to join sooner. He
was sent to Japan. He never would talk about it
either. The thing I remember best was the swords
he sent back. I showed them to all the kids in
the neighborhood. They were really thrilled.
When I was fourteen or fifteen, I was looking
for something in my mom's ceader chest, that was
where she kept all her papers. I found these
Court Marshal papers. I sat down and read the
whole transcript of the trial. My brother and
these two other guys were at this train station
and the two guys he was with beat up this Japa-

nese guy. The witnesses said my brother did not
do anything but he still got six months, in jail.
I could not understand how they could do that.
Wow that must of been awful. I ask my mom and
dad about it and ask Jim, but none of them wanted to talk about it.

Jim, Bob and I sat watching a baseball game
on t.v. Everyone else left, we were the only
one's that liked ball games. I can remember sitting and watching ball games with Jim and Bob
all through my life.

"Sharon."

"Ya, Bob."

"Don't join the army. In the first place
that's the worst branch there is. In the second
place the only women that are in the service are
old bags that can't find a husband or there weir-
d'os."

"Besides kid, when you get put on k.p. and
have to peal a 100 spuds you aren't going to
like it. You don't work around home so you sure
aren't gonna like that."

"I help my mom, Jim."

"You know, when you get in there you can't
get out, whether you like it or not."

"Jim, no one can make me do nothing!"

"Ha! that's what you think, there will be
things you have to do all your life, you don't
want to, hu Bob?"

"Jims right Sharon, so if your smart you
won't join the service."

"Sharon, you better listen to your brothers,
and I know about it too, because I was in the
Horse Marines and they sure as hell didn't mess
around with you. By God you did what you were
told and I'm telling you, you aren't gonna make
it in there. You won't get out of bed in the mornings and don't like anyone telling you what to
do, so how the hell you gonna make it in the service?"

"She's going to have to learn the hard way
pop. So Sharon just remember we told you."

I listened to them but it was to late now and besides I didn't believe everything they said. The girls at the recruiting office weren't old bags. I was sworn in that day. I raised my right hand with four other girls and we all said the words, and stood there in front of the flag and promised to do our best for our country. We got our pictures taken and they would appear in our town papers. We were given our orders and told to be at the Oakland Airport at 8:00 p.m. that night, July 26, 1960. I was in the Army.

Janice came over and told me she had to talk to me, so we went in the bedroom. I was thinking she would tell me how much she was going to miss me and maybe how much she cared for me.

"Sharon, I have to tell you something."

"O.k., Jan."

"Well I wasn't ever going to tell you this but beings your going in the service, I think I better tell you."

"What do you want to tell me Jan?"

"Well, in this world there are people that like there own sex. Homosexual or lesbian, they have bars they go to and they use this code word for it, "Gay". There is a butch and fem, the butch makes love to the fem. So now you know, thats what I wanted to tell you. I know your not like that but in the service you might meet some-one like that."

I wanted to touch Jan I loved her so much. I wanted to tell her how I felt about her and I wanted her more than anything and I didn't care what it was called. I was glad that there were other people like that and I didn't feel so al-one. Why did I have to find out all this when I was leaving?

"Jan how did you know about it?"

"Never mind I just know and I thought you bet-ter know."

My mom came in and she looked mad. She told me that I should talk to the rest of them and not just stay in there talking to Jan all night.

June ask me to sit by her, she said she wanted
to talk to me about something.

"Sharon, we all tryed to talk you out of join-
ing the service, but your so hard headed. Your
going to have to watch out for manish women in
there. There a lot of fairies in the service and
out too. I worked with some fairies. They seemed
nice but I never was alone with one of them.
That is what I have been worried about, and I
know your mom and dad are too."

"She's right Sharon."

Wow, Jan felt like June did. I felt so confused. My dad was drunk and he said some things
to June and she started crying and left with Jim.
Everything was going wrong and I had to leave,
and I was feeling worse about it. We got in the
car and Jan was sitting next to me. I watched
our house slowly disappear and I felt the tears
behind my eye lids and I hoped I could remember
what my house looked like. Jans body was warm
next to mine and I wanted to touch her so much.
She just sat there and didn't say anything. Wow,
this wasn't anything like I thought it was going
to be, she was probably glad I was going.

We got to the Airport mom, dad, Kerry, Billie,
Jan and I. Billie was crying and looked so sad.
Jan never said one word, she acted like she did-
n't even care about me at all. Then we were told
to get on the plain. I kissed everyone good by
and Jan just stood there and acted like she did-
n't even care. I turned around and started toward the plain. I heard these screams.

"Sharon, Sharon, wait, don't go Sharon!"

Jan through her arms around me and was crying
and kissing me. My dad pulled us apart and pushed me,

"Get on that plain!"

I started walking toward the plain and I kept
looking back. Jan was leaning on the fence crying and I was crying too. I got in the plain but
I couldn't see out the window. I had to sit on
the other side of the plain. I sat there and I

89

never felt so alone in all my life. My Jan did love me, and I was leaving.

I sat there and watched Oakland and San Francisco and all the beautiful blurry lights that looked like fallen stars, fading from view. I tryed to bring back the reality of Jans kisses but nothing seemed real. The girl sitting next to me was crying and she said she was scared. She ask me if I would change seats with her because she was afraid, she was sitting next to the emergency exit. I changed seats with her and she finally quit crying.

We had been in the air a couple of hours when this real bad storm started. The lightening cut through the night and the thunder sounded and the plain shook. The girl next to me started throwing up in this little bag they had on the back of the seat. They should of had a bigger bag cause that one wasn't big enough. The other girls were doing the same thing and it made me sick but I didn't through up. I thought that maybe if the plain crashed we wouldn't have to go to Ft. McClellan.

We got to Dallas Texas and when we got off the plain I couldn't breath. It was this awful hot and I just barely made it to this building. They had this moving belt thing that carried you to this restaurant part of the place. That belt was just flat, it wasn't one of thoes escalators because they went up stairs. I don't know what it was. Wow, I never seen anything like that. The five of us went in this restaurant and ordered something to eat. We had these tickets that payed for what ever we got. The thing I remember most was I ask for a large glass of milk and they brought me this little tiny glass of milk. I told the girls I was with, I thought everything was supose to be bigger in Texas.

When we got to Birmingham Alabama and got on the bus going to Ft. Mc Clellen I looked out the window. Everything was so strange. I kept thinking, I never saw so many different ways, eyes,

90

noses, and mouths could be put together. Everywhere I looked all I saw was strangers.

Alabama was a funny place there it was summer
and everything was green. We got to Ft. Mc Clel-
lan and drove through the gate. Inside it looked
like a giant golf coarse with all these three
story buildings setting neatly all over it. We
drove down this street of buildings and pulled
up in back of the next to the last one. All
these girls had there heads hanging out the wind-
dows and were yelling,

"Look, at the new recruits, ha,ha."

"What your recruiting officer tell you, you
shouldn't believed her. You'll be sorry."

We got our suitcases and this sergeant told
us to follow her. We went up to the top floor
and walked into this big room with all these
beds in it. The sergeant told us to get a bunk.
There was about five girls sitting down at the
end of the room and they were looking at us, and
one of them pointed at me and they all laughed.
Wow, I didn't like that. If this army didn't
start getting better, I wasn't going to like it.
The girl that sat next to me on the plain was in
the bunk next to me and the other three were in
the bunks next to hers. Her name was Patricia
Apodaca. I ask her if I could call her Ap short
for her last name. She said o.k.

I had to go to the bathroom but I didn't know
where it was. I ask Ap and she, ask this other
girl. They said it was out in the hall. I walked
up and down the hall but didn't see any bathroom.
All there was, was something called the latrine.
It sounded like maybe they kept there medicine
there or something. Two girls were walking down
the hall so I said,

"Hay, you guys know where the bathroom is?"

"Your standing right in front of it."

"Where?"

"Right there."

"I guess the latrine, was the bathroom."

About then this woman in a uniform came walking up to me and looked real mad.

"Are you the one that was yelling?"

"Ya."

"Yes! What did you say?"

"I ask them guys where the bathroom was?"

"There are no guys in the womans army corps, and it is yes not ya. Recruit you better watch it."

"Ya-er yes, a I will."

"Carry on."

Wow this was really something. Man I guess you weren't even going to be able to talk. I walked in the latrine and there was this row of showers with no curtains. If they think I'm going to take a shower in front of anyone there crazy. I sure don't want to be around any naked girls either. Sharon, you really did it. Wow what are you going to do? At least the bathroom had doors on it. I went back inside the room and was walking to my bunk when some one yelled,

"Don't walk down the middle isle."

"Hu?"

"Don't walk down that middle isle it's off limits."

"Oh, o.k."

There was this middle isle with tall lockers on each side of it and you weren't supose to walk on it. Wow, this place was really something. Lights out was at 10:00 and I waited until the lights were out before I got dressed and got in bed. Thoes girls laughed again. All of a sudden I heard all this beautiful singing. It was the Lords Prayer and it seemed to be echoing to us right from heaven. You could hear four or five choirs of angels singing softly until you couldn't keep from crying and then this lonely trumpet that sounded a million miles away played it's sad and lonely song. The sergeant opened the door and said in a soft voice,

"It's our tradition around here to sing the Lords Prayer every evening before taps."

I woke up with lights in my face and some one

92

shaking me.

"Sharon, get up the sergeants already been hear twice."

"O.k. thanks Ap. What time is it anyway?"

"It's quater after 5:00."

Oh wow, I got up and got dressed and brushed my teeth and then we went down stairs and we had to stand outside all lined up for reveille. All the platoons were out there and they looked so sharp. They stood so proud and then they raised the flag and the trumpet played. Then we had to march up to the mess hall. Wow, that marching is really something I kept getting stepped on from behind and stepping on the person in front of me. Boy, I didn't know if I could ever learn to march and the sergeant kept giving me dirty looks. Well, I never marched before. "Heft, heft, heft, right, heft."

We stood in line for what seemed like a hour. We got these trays and walked down this line un- til we came to the steam tables where the cooks placed a certain amount and kind of food in our

steal trays. Then we were told where to sit. I
sat at a table with four people I didn't even
know. The food was a mess, maybe that's why they
called it the mess hall. I didn't feel hungry
anyway. When we got back to the barricks. Every
one was smiling. We stood in line and got advan-
ced $40.00. We got this list of stuff we were
supose to buy and we were going to be taken to
the P.X. That was the most money I ever had in
my life. I just kept looking at it. It kind of
scared me having that much money.

We got back from the P.X. with irons, soap,
brasso, shoe polish and all kinds of stuff. We
didn't have very much money left after buying
all that stuff on the list. Then we were marched
to this warehouse to be issued our uniforms. We
stood in line while all these cloths were piled
in our arms. They got mad at me because I didn't
know what size I wore. Well my mom never told me.
They measured us for our dress greens. That was
our class A uniform. We were told we were among
the first to get the green uniform. Then we had
to take all our civilian cloths and put them
down stairs in the basement and that was when I
found out in the Woman's Army Corps they did not
allow levis or pants of any kind. That was when
I was really ready to walk all the way back to
California.

The platoon was filled up and we were called
B-2 short for company B, second platoon and we
were going to start our schooling right away. We
were learning to make a bed the army way and had
night details (everyone had a cleaning job) and
had to arange all our cloths just a certain way
and polish our shoes just so. We had old ladies
high heels they called granies, and these ankel
boots they called little abners. In basic training we would only wear these P.T. cloths. P.T.
cloths were a brown skirt and blouse and of
course our little abners with brown socks. Well,
Sharon you ask for it.

94

Chapter Twelve

There wasn't enough hours in the day. We got up at 5:00 am every morning, stood reveille, went to breakfast then came back to the barricks. We had to make our beds with folded corners and take this blanket and fix, what they called a hood over the pillow. The white

bed was the worst. We had to have exactly a 6 inch cuff on the bed. They measured it with a ruler. They had a diagram of where all our cloths were supose to be in our foot locker and wall locker. All our shoes were lined up under our bed and we used Pledge on the out side of our lockers and got on our hands and knees and polished the floor all around our bed. You got gigs or demerits for dust. Our cloths had to be washed, starched and ironed every night. That was really hard because the whole platoon had to use only four ironing boards and we usely had to iron our cloths wet in order to get done before lights out. We also had details to do every night and polish our shoes and brass.

You weren't supose to have any wrinkles in your skirt. We had to learn how to sit in our skirts without getting wrinkles in it. We went to school from 7:00 a.m. to 4:00 p.m. with a half hour for lunch. They called lunch dinner and then dinner was supper, and at lunch they had the largest meal, everything was so confusing. I got a letter from Jan. She said for me to remember everything I knew she taught me. She said all the girls on the ball team said that I wouldn't feel the same about her when I came back home. She said she told them that wasn't true. I couldn't change my feelings about Jan.

I really loved her.

I hated school worse than anything. You had
to sit there and keep awake and couldn't lean on
your elbows or anything. You had to have both
feet on the floor and sit erect with your shoulders back. They would come around with a ruler
and hit you if you leaned on your elbow or did-
n't have your feet flat on the floor. It was so
hard keeping awake, I was always so tired. If
you were caught with your eyes closed you had to
stand up in back of the class for the rest of
the hour.

We had to learn all the Army patches and
ranks. We had to learn how to slute all officers.
We had to learn to walk and stand all these correct table manners. Wac's were ladies and had to
conduct thereselves above reproch. We had what
they called troop information, where they told
us about the trouble in Laos. They showed us a
film on brain washing and told about how awful
the communists were. We couldn't read no news papers or listen to any radios. It was really awful.

I never knew I was so sloppy. I got more gigs
than anyone. Inspections were really something.
We use to want a cigarette so bad but we could-
n't dirty a ash tray because we would get giged
for it. So we would take a kleen X and put our
ashes in it and then squash the cigarette out in
the kleen X and then put them in our bra's. At
the last minute before inspection all U.O.'s
(unourtherised objects) lint, papers anything we
would get giged for went in our bra's. We had to
stand at least a hour and a half every Saterday
morning for inspection. It was really hard and
some girls passed out and they really got in
trouble. No one was supose to pass out that was
a order. You stood there at parade rest with
your eyes straight ahead. If you moved your eyes
you got giged. I thought that was rotten.

"What have we here Recruit Davis? Twelve U.O.'s
thought you could hide your candy papers hu? Re-

cruit, the bottom of your statenary box is not
for candy papers."

"Yes mame."

"Recruit Isabell, if you don't start emprov-
ing you'll spend your whole basic in the barricks without a pass."

"Yes, mame."

"Attend-hut! This platoon needs work, lots of
work!"

"Dismissed!"

We all started getting ready for the parade.
After inspection was the parade. Oh that was
really awful. All the Companies marched up the
hill to the parade grounds. It was so hot and
you could see the backs of every ones uniforms
were all wet. If someone passed out you were
supose to keep marching. One girl fell and cracked her head open. I thought the Army was rotten,
we weren't even human beings. I wouldn't treat
anyone the way they were treating us.

We stood for a hour or more in the hot sun
while these officers talked. You couldn't move
except when ordered. When we marched passed the
reviewing stand and the sergeant said,

"Eyes right."

Wow, you couldn't help but feel proud, all
those officers standing there and the flags and
bands playing. You know what happened to me.
This dam bee flew on my nose. Honest to god. I
couldn't knock it off or anything and I guess
that was about the hardest part. I had a real awful time walking in those granies. They had
thick heels but I would be marching and all of a
sudden I'd be walking on the side of my foot.
When I was a kid they wanted to put braces on my
legs because my feet were so crooked but my mom
and dad said it wouldn't do no good because I
wouldn't wear them. My dad use to make me walk
by him all the time and he would hit me and tell
me to straighten my feet out.

K.P. was really something, you worked from
4:00 a.m. until sometimes 8:00 at night and

still had all your other work. I never seen so
many pots and pans in my life and they were so
big. We scrubed the whole kitchen after every
meal. The cook was emtying these big cans of
fruit cocktail in this pan. The pan slipped and
everything fell in the garbage pan. "Can't let
all that go to waste." She scraped that fruit
cocktail out of the garbage pail. I never ate
any fruit cocktail again.

They had what they called policeing, you had
to walk down the streets picking up papers and
what made me sick was when we had to pick these
old wet cigarette buts out of these but cans.
(outside ash trays.) I was really getting mad.

"How can they do this to us, boy if someone
found out I bet they would get in trouble."

"They have to teach us discipline Isabell, it
just makes it harder on yourself thinking like
that. You act like a little kid."

We went to church every Sunday. That was really strange. I didn't know much about church. My
dad said anyone that went to church was a hypo-
crite if they didn't do everything the bible
said. That ment not smoking or cussing or drinking, and being good. I felt guilty going to
church, I smoked and wasn't good.

Lt. Young our platoon officer played the or-
gan in church. She was really beautiful. She was
this soft velvet black and every movement she
made was so sharp and proud. She had the best
slute of anyone I ever saw in the army. She was
so tiny, but when she walked it was just like a
general, I never saw anyone so fine in my life.
She always wore this good smelling perfume too.
I could have just looked at her for hours.

All of us really were close working together
and not knowing if we could stand it. Those were
the most honorable fine women I ever met and we
really loved our country and wanted to be good
Wacs. Our song was,

"Duty is calling you and me, we have a date
with destiny, ready the Wacs are ready, there

98

pulse is steady a world to set free. Service, were in it heart and soul, victory is our only goal. We love our Countrys honor and we'll uphold it against any foe."

Anything, anyone did effected every one. So we all had to stick together to make it. I didn't want to do anything to hurt my platoon but I was so depressed and mad. I knew I was letting every one down, I had to get away from there. So I got my levis from down stairs and figered out how I was going to run away. I left a letter telling them I was sorry. I only had ten dollars but even if I had to walk all the way back to Calif. I was leaving. I waited until everyone was asleep and then I went down the back stairs and I crawled for about a half mile between the barricks. I started running and then I came to this fence about eight feet high. I got over it and started walking away from the road. I walked about ten miles when I figered it would probably be safe. I'd never make it to Calif. unless I hitch hiked. I looked like a boy and I cut my hair even shorter than it was, so they wouldn't know I was a girl and catch me. Well the second car that came by was the cops.

"Hay boy, where you going so late."
"Up the road."
"Get in the car. Where's your I.D?"
"I don't have one."
"You run off from the army boy, didn't you?"
"No."
"Were taking you back to the fort."

Every one was really disapointed in me. I gave my platoon a bad name and I didn't have any guts and what I did made it worse for everyone.

"Isabell, you could really be a top Wac. Every one believed in you and you messed up. We laughed at you at first but when we got to know you we really felt bad about that. When you said we ought to have a meeting and get together and work to make it we all thought that was really something. You let everyone down, you really did."

I wished I was dead. I got a artical 15. The
Captain said she should Court Marshall me. I had
an extra detail every night. I waxed the whole
bottom floor and buffed it with a kotex pad.
Scrubed the stairs with a tooth brush. Cleaned
Lt. Youngs office every night. They said they
weren't going to send me to the head shrinker.
Wow I had so much work.

We learned about germ warfare and we had to
learn all about wearing gas masks. They took us
in this building and set off some tear gas. We
had to stay in there with our gas mask on then
the sergeant made us take the gas mask off and
give our name rank and serial number. Everyone
came out crying. Then we had to go in there and
they set off chocking gas and we had to pull our
masks off and put them on again. The sergeant
told us to hold our breath and not to breath any
of the gas. One girl couldn't get her mask on
and she started chocking. They took her outside.

We could go out on the rifle range if we wanted to and I hit a bulls eye. We were getting
ready to go on biv-wac. I got my first pass to
town. I didn't even want to go. They had given
us this big lecture about following the town
rules when we went there. They said we couldn't
do anything about it. So me and my Black friends
couldn't walk down the street together. My
friends couldn't go in the same restaurant,
drink out of the same fountain or use the same
bathroom. After we had been through hell together. I sat in the back of the bus and I didn't
care if they put me in jail. I liked sitting in
the back of the bus. It made me sick, the whole
stinken mess. Treating human beings like animals,
hurten people, I didn't like that I knew what it
was like to be hurt and I don't ever want to
hurt anyone.

I found out when Lt. Young was in Officers
School, it was located there on the post, they
had this picnic for graduation. They decided to
go to this park in town. Those people said Lt.

Young was the finest person I ever knew. How could people be like that?

We were going on biv-wac. That ment we got to ware these combat cloths and go out in the feild for two days. Combat cloths were pants, ha, ha. I sure liked getting out of a dam dress even if just for two days. That day they marched us down this road and told us to give first aid to anyone in front of us or behind us that pretended they had something wrong with them. This one girls started screaming and climbing this telephone poll. It scared me, it seemed real. That night they marched us down this road and all of a sudden this plain flew over and droped something. We were told to put on our gas masks and hit the ditches. Frances was crying and I put my arm around her. She grabed my shirt and held on to me. We slep in tents that night and they had infultrators trying to get through the night guards and you could hear them all night.

"Halt, who goes there."

"Halt, who goes there. Advance and be recognized."

The next day they said there was an envasion and then these plains started flying over us again dropping things. Girls were falling over and we were supose to give them first aid. I just stood there and I couldn't move. I couldn't move, I just couldn't move.

A milatary graduation is really something. All proud and you march up in line and slute and shake hands when you get your diploma. We were all going to different parts of the country, to different schools or posts. The tearful good bys were said, but we all marched out with our heads high we were B-2 and we were Wacs.

Me and five other girls were going to stay there. We were going to the clerical school there on post. All through basic everyone prayed that wouldn't happen to them. That was supose to be the worst thing that could happen to you.

We were marched up the hill to C.T.C. and

were told we had to do policeing details until our new platoon filled up. Me and Abbott were out chopping weeds when the Sergeant walked up and told us to report in Class A uniforms to Head and Head. That was the Officers school.

"Wow, Abbott what do you think they want us over there for?"

"I don't know, it must not be a detail if we have to wear our class A's."

They were making a moving picture and me and Abbott were going to be second Lt.'s. No kidding, there we were in a moving picture and for three days we walked around with Lt. bars on our shoulders with everyone sluting us. Lt. Young was in the movie too. She said can you emagin this, these two women were recruits in my platoon just a few days ago and now there Lt.'s. That was really a strange experience. I didn't like having people slute me. I knew what they were going through and how they felt.

Classes started and I hated it. I didn't like clerical school. We still had all the inspections and the parades. I just waited and hoped I would get stationed, in California. I was so home sick and I missed Jan so much. In the letters I received everyone sounded like they were having a good time. Well graduation finally came for the third time in one year. I received a B average in school. I don't know how that happened. I put in for a fifteen day leave. After graduation we went in the day room and waited for our orders. Five girls were being sent to Calif. My name was the last one on the list, that they read.

"Isabell, to Ft. Leanard Wood Mo."

Well, I had fifteen days before I reported to Ft. Leanard Wood. It had been four months sence I had been home. I bought a bus ticket for Calif. I didn't have enough money for anything else and I had saved my money too. We received $78.00 a month. California here I come.

102

Chapter Thirteen

I bought my bus ticket.
I got a discount on the
price, because I was in
uniform. I was invited
to go with some of the
girls to New York and
to New Orleanes, but
all I could think of
was California. I was
on the bus for three
days and three nights.
I sat up and slept and

tryed to be careful not to wrinkle my uniform.
In Mississippi I met this real nice old lady.
Her name was Mrs. White. She was very interested
in the Women's Service and ask me a bunch of
questions. She wanted to lend me some money so I
could fly home. I couldn't eccept because I did
not know if I could pay her back. I met this guy
that had been living in Mexico. He was a beech
comber. He was a very interesting person.

I had to buy some lipstick because you weren't
supose to be in uniform without lipstick. There
was these boys about eighteen or nineteen standing by the counter. One of them threw his emty
cigarette package at me. I felt like sluging him
but I was a Wac, so I just held my head up and
walked off.

I did not think I would ever get to Calif. I
thought that all the other states I went through
couldn't even compare with Calif. I could not understand how anyone could live anywhere else.
When I got to Oakland I started crying and cryed
all the way to Concord. I was so glad to be home
and I was so sorry for ever saying one bad thing
about my home.

I called Jan and ask her to come and get me
at the bus station. She came in the bus station
and through her arms around me and said she was
glad to see me,

"I'm sure glad to see you. You really look
nice in your uniform."

"Thanks Jan."

I did not know what it was but there was something changed between us. She looked so different. She told me all the latest news about everyone. Betty had her baby. Helen got married. All
the guys are in the service and most of the
girls are married.

Jan had changed so much and it seemed her
softness was gone. It seemed that a lot of feelings were gone. I didn't understand, and I did
not want to believe what I was thinking and feeling. My mom was mad at me because I had Jan come
and get me instead of her. When my dad saw me he
started crying. I couldn't stand to see him cry.

I would only be able to spend ten days at
home because of the traveling time. I went up to
the school and saw my teachers. Mrs. Benson was
one of my favorite teachers and she ask me to
have some coffee with her in the teachers lounge.
Wow that sure seemed funny sitting there drinking coffee with a teacher. Mrs. Benson was a
great teacher. Mr. Cassel was another great teacher. I admired him very much. I'll never forget
a year before the election of Pres. Kennedy, how
he predicted he would win. Everybody didn't believe him because most people had never heard of
Pres. Kennedy then. My recruiting officer said
my teachers really gave me excellent references.
I did not think they would.

All the time I was home I felt so depressed
because I did not want to go to Ft. Leanard Wood.
I would have to leave a week before Christmas
too. Everyone acted like I was really somebody
because I was in the service.

Jan told me she was gay and she had always
been gay. I think I loved and hated her at the
same time. She said there had always just been
friendship between us. She said I was not gay. I
knew that wasn't true. The last night I was home,
I was going to spend the night with Jan but my

mom and dad wouldn't let me. I really got mad
and yelled at them and they said the Army sure
didn't help me to grow up any.

My mom and dad took me to the Oakland bus station. I felt so dead inside and so lonely and
lost. I got on the bus and I watched California
leave mile by mile. I remembered the last ten
days. I was so glad I could remember. I thought
the most beautiful thing in the world was a mem-
ory.

I thought Missouri was ugly. When the bus en-
tered the main gate to the Fort, there was this
row of crosses along the road. "So many have
died here, speed kills." All I saw was three
story brown and green buildings. No grass anywhere just dirt. The bus pulled up in front of
the Wac Detatchment and I got off the bus. This
would be my home for twenty months. I sat my
suitcase down and then sat on it and began to
cry. I was crying so much it scared me and I
thought maybe I couldn't stop. Finally I went inside of the orderly room. I walked up to the sergeant major.

"Pvt Isabell reporting as ordered."

"Sit down pvt. I'll send the supply sergeant
to show you where your quarters will be."

The supply sergeant gave me some blankets and
things and then took me to the barricks. It was
dirty brown inside and out. It was heated with
coal. You would wake up in the morning with soot
all over you and your bed. My room had two bunks,
two foot lockers, two wall lockers and one dresser. There were five of these rooms with a isle
down the middle. Twenty of us all living together. It was dark and emty and the supply sergeant
said most of the women were on leave for Christmas.

"Mitchell, you got a new room mate."

"Hi, whats your name?"

"Sharon."

I sat down on my bunk and started crying a-
gain.

"Hey, everything will seem better when you get use to it."

"Thank you."

"I have to go to the P. X. do you want to go with me? Maybe you would feel better."

"O.K."

We walked up the hill and I saw this armed guard. Mitchell told me they had a twenty four hour a day, watch around the Wac Detatchment to keep guys from trying to go in the Wac barricks. There were 10,000 men and 100 women there.

We got to the P. X. and I bought some soap and cigarettes and waited by the door for Mitchell. This sergeant walked in and took the door and through it back and it hit me and knocked me down. He gave me a dirty look and walked off. Wow, that was really mean. I felt like crying again.

The next day I was taken to my new job. I was a receptionist in the hospital. My boss a sergeant major said he didn't like Wac's and they were always sending them to him.

There was this guy that worked there and his nick name was ham. He showed me where everything was and told me jokes. He was really nice. I was the only one in the office that worked Christmas. I worked from 7:00 a.m. to 8:00 p.m. those were my regular working hours. I worked 10 days and then had three days off. I had Christmas dinner in the hospital cafeteria. There wasn't very many people there and I felt sorry for everyone that was. I don't believe I have ever been so lonely and depressed in my life.

New years I felt bad but not as bad as I did at Christmas. I was just going to stay there and feel sorry for myself and that was getting to be quite a habit. This girl named Marg came in and sat down. She was really something, she would always come in and talk to Mitchell. She had been living with this guy and this girl. She said she couldn't make up her mind which one she loved. She said she liked to jack off the guy.

She said she must have a penis envy complex or something. She also set around reading Time magmagazine all the time and her I.Q. was 130. She said I acted like I was retarted or something.

"Hey, kid your comming out with me."

"I don't want to go out."

"Look you have to do something, your really a dud. I never seen anyone that was such a mess. You just sit around all the time like your retarted. I bet you've never done nothing or been anywhere in your life before you came in the service."

"I guess not."

"Get dressed your going with me."

I got dressed and we went to the bus station and then went about five miles down the road to this strip of bars. We got off the bus and walked up to this bar. This man had this woman against this car beating her up. I wanted to try and stop it.

"Look, stupid. Don't stick your nose in to something that isn't any of your business."

We went inside the bar and there was a fight going on in there. Marg laughed and acted like nothing was happening. This guy came up and ask me to dance. I said no and Marg said yes and told the guy to go ahead and dance with me. Then she said, "your on your own," and walked off.

There I was in that strange place with a strange person. I was really scared. The guy I was with was a nice guy and he took me back to the barricks. I didn't like that bar. Marg came in late that night singing and really drunk. She came over to my bed and said,

"I forgot to give you a New years kiss."

She kissed me and then left.

Marg came over to my room the next day. She just sat and looked at me and I started getting all these feelings. I was scared but I kissed her.

"Well, it sure took you long enough to do

that."

Then we started making out and I wanted to
make love to her. I didn't know how. I was really upset too.

"Take it easy kid, there's more than kissing,
lot's more."

She started making love to me. I wished I
could make love to her. Her hands were gental
and soft and her mouth was on my chest. All of a
sudden I wanted to jump up and run. My body was
cold and I didn't want anyone to touch me. I
just layed there and she stopped,

"I should know better than to mess with a kid."

She kissed me and left.

This guy at work ask me out. He was short and
heavy set and a little guy about thirty. I
thought he looked like a safe nice guy. His name
was Levon. He took me to this quiet little bar
and we were sitting there and my favorite song
was playing, "Wonder Land By Night." I started
thinking about Jan and home and was feeling very
depressed. I started drinking, Singapore Slings.
Then he said he wanted to take me to this special place. We drove to this big night club.
There was a large cover charge, and the place
was packed but there was only me and two other
girls in the whole place. There was this big
stage and a piano. I sat there drinking more
Singapore Slings. This real pretty woman came
out on the stage in a real sexy black dress.

"Watch this Sharon, just watch, she's going
to strip."

"I don't believe you, your just saying that."

The woman started danceing around and then
she took off one glove and through it to the
howling, whistling croud of men. Then she took
off her other glove.

"Thats it, she's not going to do it."

"Just watch you'll see."

She unzipped her dress and I was embarrassed.
I didn't want to look. I tryed not to look. She
had everything off. She had these two little
108

things covering her nipples and this little
string with a patch over her private part. She
stood up there and moved like she was having intercourse and the men were yelling and reaching
for her and one guy jumped up and started taking
his pants down. Someone stopped him. I told Levon I was leaving. He got mad. He took me back
to the Wac Detatchment and I started to get out
of the car and he grabed me and started kissing
me and getting fresh. I told him to leave me a-
lone and I got out of the car.

The guys use to come by my desk at work and
talk to me. Four different guys ask me to marry
them. This one night I was getting off work at
8:00 and this guy that had been trying to get me
to go out with him was waiting in the hall. I
walked passed him and started for the door. He
grabed me and pushed me against the wall and he
had me pinned in the corner. He started pulling
at my cloths and kissing me. I was so scared and
I told him to stop. I started screaming and he
put his hand over my mouth. Tommy my black
friend saw what was happening and she came in
and was real mad.

"What are you doing! You let her go!
"Come on Sharon, were going home."

She really saved me. I sure was lucky, she
just happened to be working late and walked by.

I met this guy named troy. He was nice and we
use to go to this restaurant and eat cheese sandwitches and laugh and talk. He told me he was
gay and I told him I thought that was wonderful
because I was too. He said he thought I might be.
He told me that when guys first have intercourse
they blead just like women. He said almost everyone in his barricks was gay, or having af-
fairs. He told me about him and this guy making
love in a sleeping bag when they were out in the
feild.

We went for a walk and troy ask me to make
love to him. I told him I liked women. He said,
"Pretend I'm a woman."

109

"How can I pretend, your just not like a woman."

"Well try."

I started feeling his body but it wasn't soft. We were standing in this forest. When I got to his private parts I stopped. He went over and sat on this stump and started masturbating, he ask me to do it for him. I tryed but I didn't like it and he said I wasn't doing it right. He explained about how it was done. Then it went off. All this stuff shot out. I couldn't understand what Marg saw in jacking a guy off.

Troy said he was in love with me and gave me this ring and said he wanted to marry me. I didn't feel anything for him but friendship and I told him. The next night one of Troys friends came over and told me he went A.W.O.L. because I wouldn't marry him. The guy said that if he could tell Troy I cared about him maybe he could get him to come back. I told him I cared about Troy. Troy and I were supose to get married. I thought maybe if I was married I could get out of the service.

I wanted to get drunk. So I tryed to find someone to go with me. This girl said she'd go with me. I didn't know her but I didn't want to be alone. We went to the N.C.O. club and I ordered beer with a triple chaser of whiskey. I sat there getting really drunk. This guy came over and the girl and him started danceing and talking. Then she said this guy would give us a ride back to the barricks. She said she knew the guy so I said O.K. Another guy was waiting in the car. I said I wasn't going with them. They told me I was really silly. So I got in the car. I was really drunk. They drove out somewhere and parked. The guy, the girl was with got a blanket and they got out of the car. The guy I was with came over and started kissing me and trying to get freash.

"Look! Wait until your friend gets through with her and then take your turn but leave me
110

alone."

"O.k. I will."

Both the guys had intercourse with the girl
and then they took us back to the barricks. I never been so upset in my life and I had to talk
to someone so I told one of the girls about it.

"Didn't you know about her. Wow, she works in
the motor pool and she let ten guys get to her,
one right after another. She's getting kicked
out of the service."

It seemed like I was always getting into something. I wish I knew how to get out of the Army.
Well April 15, 1961, I was supose to be getting
married.

Chapter Fourteen

I can remember stand-
ing outside of the bar-
ricks and looking at
the long slinder ici-
cles hanging from the
roofs edges. Some of
the icicles were so
long they touched the
snow covered ground.
Some of the girls had
built a snowman. I re-
membered when I was a
kid, how me and Kerry always wanted to build a
snowman. Kerry was so sweet, she sent me a letter and signed it your fighting sister. When I
read her letter I cryed, I wanted to go home so
bad. The girls said,
"Sharon, all you do is talk about home and
Janice. You won't let us get close enough to
you to be your friends."
I tryed not thinking about home and Jan but I
could not stop thinking and feeling so lonely. I
hated the Army and I could not stand seeing the
way people were being treated. They did not have
to be so mean and heartless. I was told I was
not very grown up. What is all this shit about
being grown up anyway? Does that mean you go a-
round not caring about anyone or anything? Does
that mean you start being mean to people and
pushing them around, and think inside your great.
What in the hell is wrong with me? Why do I always think different than everyone else? Why
can't I just do what everyone else does and feel
the way they do?
I got a letter from Charmaine, she was going
through basic training at Ft. McClellen. Wow, I
did not think she was going to join the service.
She never even wrote me and ask me about the service. Well I hoped she liked it better than I
did, and I hoped she would get stationed in Cal-

ifornia.

I got on the basketball team, that was a honor and not very many girls made the team. We went on T.D.Y. and did not have to go to work. We traveled all over Missouri and Kansas playing basketball. We had a very good team and we won most of the games we played. We played Army and Civilian teams. We were preparing for the Fifth Army Chapionship, which would be held at Ft. Leanard Wood.

The Fifth Army Chapionship games lasted a week and all we did was play basketball that whole week. Teams came from all the forts in the Fifth Army. The Fifth Army extended from Chicago to Denver, and I got to see some of the girls I was in basic training with, they were stationed in Denver.

Chicago had won the Chapionship for years and they were expected to win again. The tournament was really exciting and the last game was really close. When we won the whole gym was a mass of screaming happy people. We received a trophy about three feet high to be kept in our detatchment trophy case. We also received these very nice blankets imported from Oregon. We had to go to this big banquet and we had a steak dinner and saw a floor show. It was real nice and we were really happy. The mens team won the Chapionship too, so Ft. Leonard Wood was really honored.

Tammy my best friend tried to help me get a transfer to California. She had a friend at Ft. Ord California that wanted to come to Ft. Leonard Wood to be with her. I filled out the papers and was going to pay any extra expences but they would not aprove the transfer. I was really mad. I could not understand why they would not let us transfer. Some of the girls said once they get you at Ft. Leonard Wood they never let you go. They had a saying about Ft. Leonard Wood,

"If your boys to to Germany, send them money. If your boys go to Korea write them. If your

113

boys go to Ft. Leonard Wood prey for them."

A girl got pregnant and was getting descharged, they put her on K.p. until the descharge
came through. She would be lucky if she didn't
have a miscarriage. One girl had a appendicitis
attact and they took her to the hospital and
left her laying on the table for three hours,
screaming because they said she was just having
labor pains. Finally someone came in and descov-
ered her appendix was bursting and took her in
the operating room and butchered her up. She
showed me the mess they made of her stomack. She
said she was getting out of the service while
she was still alive.

Tammy was going out with some guy and she
said she found out some things about the strip
of bars outside of the fort. A big syndicate run
the strip and if she told me what she knew she
would be murdered. I told her maybe we could go
to someone and do something about it. She begged
me to just forget about it.

Well I had, had it. I was getting out of the
service. I had seen all I could stand and so I
went over to the orderly room and said I wanted
to see the Captain. I walked in her office and
said,

"Either you let me out of the Army or I'm
leaving on my own."

"Pvt! I am your cammanding officer. Do you
know you could get a court marshall for talking
to me like that!"

"I don't care, I hate the Army and I'm leaving on my own."

"Pvt. I'm going to send you to the post psychiatrist."

I went to the head shrinker and he really got
mad and said he did not even want to talk to me.
He said I was rebellious and rude. So they had
me talk to the head psychiatrist. He was very
nice and ask me a lot of questions about how I
felt about the service. I told him exactly how I
felt. He said I was not the type of person that
114

could adapt to milatary life and my rebellious
attude was very unhealthy. He said it was very
clear that I did not want to change my attude
and he thought that the service was not the
place for me and he would arange for my descharge as soon as possable. He ask me to try and
conduct myself properly until my descharge came
through.

I called my mom and told her, I was comming
home. She said,

"Sharon your just getting out because Janice
told you to. Sharon don't quit now. What will
you do when you get home? Please for me, stay
in."

I told Troy I was not going to marry him. He
really got mad and he talked and talked and tryed everything to get me to marry him. I could
not understand him. I did not know how he could
feel the way he said he felt about me. Troy told
me that if I wanted to make some money he could
arange for me to work for the syndicate. All I
had to do was fly back and forth across the country smugling dope. I told him he was full of
shit. He said he was serious and he could really arange something. I told him all I wanted to
do was go home. He said he was going to follow
me to California and one day we would be married.
Life is really weird and I didn't believe nothing Troy said, it was just unbelieveable.

They made me paint the latrine while I was
waiting for my descharge. No one would hardly
speak to me and I really felt bad. The girls
said they were going to make it without quitting
if it killed them. I felt like a crummy quiter.
Marg ask me to give her my address and phone number because she was thinking about going to California when she got out and she only had ninty
some days left.

I had to turn in all my cloths. I could not
keep them because I did not stay in my whole
time. One girl stayed her whole time and when
she got descharged she took her uniforms and put

them in a pile in the middle of the detachment
and set them on fire.

I had $190.00 back pay comming. Wow I felt
like a millionaire. I bought my bus ticket and
it cost me about $60.00 dollars. I was going to
give my mom and dad a $100.00 wow were they go-
ing to be happy. I was really scared carrying
all that money with me on the bus, I kept checking my pocket to make sure the money was still
there. I watched Ft. Leonard Wood leave my sight
and I felt like a new person. I never wanted to
see that place as long as I lived again.

I felt calm inside and I looked at all the
beautiful scenery and was so glad I was going
home. The first thing I did when I saw mom was
give her the money and she didn't want to take
it. Wow, I thought they would really be happy.
My dad ask me what I was going to do, he said I
had to find a job.

Everything had really changed. Our croud was
all split up and gone. Everyone had changed so
much. I had left a beautiful life and come back
to real emtyness. How could everything change so
much?

Jan told me all about the girls she had gone
with all through school while she was telling me
she wasn't like that. I really felt betrayed,
why couldn't she have told me what was going on,
instead of letting me think there was something
wrong with me and I was all alone. She said she
didn't think I would have understood. Now that I
was more grown up and knew we were just friends
she said she could talk to me about it.

Everyone kept asking me how come I got out of
the service so fast. I didn't know what to tell
them. I wanted to go some where and hide. I
guess I was a real disapointment to everyone. It
was awful and I didn't know what to do.

Jan was going to all these parties, she said
I couldn't go because I wasn't twentyone. She
said she was the only one under age that could
go. Finally Jan took me to my first gay bar. It

was really neat, all girls and they were playing
pool and talking and really having a good time.
Someone told that I wasn't twentyone and I got
kicked out of the bar. I couldn't get in any of
the gay girls bars so I started hanging out at
the gay boys bars. The guys really liked me and
I started making a lot of friends. They would
take me to all of the all male bars, and parties.
I was the only girl that they would take to most
of the places. They would always be going to fix
me up with there sisters. One night this guy and
I were dancing and the bar tender came over and
said for us to leave the club because the guys
weren't supose to dance. I told them I was a
girl but they wouldn't believe me. Me and the
guy started laughing, that was really something.
Most of the bars let the guys dance but that was
a new bar and they were afraid of getting closed.

I got a job working for Atomic Lab, a electronics company. I got the job through a employment agency and it cost me $245.00 dollars. I
started out at a $1.25 a hour. It took me three
months to pay for just getting the job. We make
Cloud Chambers, Rayatrons, Atomatrons, Testa
coils, and I worked at sodering, assembly and
then my boss taught me how to silk screen circuit boards. I had my own room where I make the
screens. I did the whole photographic silk
screening process by myself. I liked silk screening and my boss said I was really good at it. My
dad bought a new car and let me take over the
payments on his old car, so I had some wheels.

Charmaine was stationed in San Francisco. I
went over to visit her when she went to Stockton
for the weekend. We went down town to get a coke
and we talked all about the service and everything.

"Sharon, I have something I want to tell you,
but you have to promise not to tell anyone."

"I want to tell you something too Charmaine."

"You first Sharon."

"No, you first."

117

"Well, I was really in love with this guy and I went to bed with him and now I've found out I'm pregnant, and I'm getting discharged from the service. I don't know what I'm going to do, my mothers going to kill me. I'm going to have to figure out something, oh what was you going to tell me?"

"I'm a queer, how's that grab you?"

"You know I always thought you might be. Haven't you met any guys you like? Sharon when I get over this I'm going to take you out and interduce you to some nice guy and get you over this queer business."

Charmaine said she was going to try and get her grandmother to help her and she would write and tell me everything. I promised that I wouldn't tell anyone about her being pregnant.

My sister Billie was living in a project in Pittsburg. She was living in county houseing, and was still on welfare. She wanted to paint the inside of her house, so I went over and helped her. Billie couldn't paint very good so I did most of it. We were painting and drinking beer and laughing when Billie went to the door to see who pulled up in the drive way.

"I'll be go to hell, it's Chester B. Willson."

"What!"

Sure enough after four years her husband pulled up in the drive way and walked in the house. I wanted to slug him in the mouth. My sister had been through hell for four years. He had left four years ago and went to florida and signed on a shrimp boat. He traveled all over and went to South America and saw the slave boats that were still running a big slave trade. He said the guys called him the old man of the sea. I guess he saw some pretty awful things but I didn't think it was right the way he left Billie. He wouldn't say one word or anything. I come right out and told him I thought he was dam rotten and he didn't know what my sister had been through. He went and got another six pack of beer and we

118

sat there talking and he saw his son Mike for
the first time. Oh shit this world is so dam complicated, I must be retarted like Marg said, because I am beginning to really think I don't understand life, or people. Billie and Chester got
back together and he got a job and with in five
months my sister was pregnant.

Janice and I got an apartment in Concord with
a swimming pool. She had a job dog grooming. She
made more money than I did. We were living together as friends even tho I didn't care much
for the friend bit, but I was getting use to the
idea, I didn't have much of a choice.

I went over to the bars in Oakland about every week end. This one night some of the guys
introduced me to this woman and we all went to
her apartment. There were four gay guys and she
and I. I kept thinking, here was my chance to
make love to a woman for the first time. I had
thought of exactly how I was going to do it. We
were sitting there and all of a sudden she started kissing me. Wow I was supose to be making
love to her,

"Hey wait a minute, I'm supose to be the
butch."

"Well be one, but don't just sit there."

We were really making out and then the guys
said they were going to leave us lovers alone
and go over to there place and do some love making there selves. Soon as they left she started
taking her cloths off. Wow, I just stood there.
Then she started taking my shirt off. Wow, I did-
n't like that and then she grabed my pants and I
fell off the bed. Wow this wasn't anything like
I thought about. After all my cloths was off she
layed down on the bed and wispered for me to
come to her. I was scared but I wanted her and
it made me hot looking at her laying there. I
went over to her and when our bodies touched it
was the warmest exciting thing I had ever felt.
I started feeling like I couldn't breath and I
couldn't say anything. I touched her soft shoul-

119

ders and her back and her breasts were all swollen with excitment and I started shaking all over. I kept running my hands over her body and kissing her neck and her shoulders, and then my mouth was on and all around her breast. My mouth and hands touched and kissed every part of her and I was surrounded with warmth and softness and her sounds and murmurs made me tremble and she pulled me even closer to her.

I didn't want it to ever end, it was really beautiful and I loved kissing and touching her. Then in a wave of soft jerking movements it was over and we layed there in each others arms and I kept touching her gently. Then there was a knock at the door, someone calling her.

"It's my husband!"

"Your husband, wow I didn't know you were married."

"Get your cloths on, hurry."

I never moved so fast in my life, I could just see us getting our heads blown off. Sharon, why do you always get yourself in messes like this? She opened the door and this guy walked in and they started yelling at each other and then she picked up a vace and through it at him. I was scared and I started walking toward the door, then she started cussing at me. All I could think of was getting out of there I didn't know she was married. I started walking off and then the husband came up to me and ask me if I wanted to go and have a beer with him. Wow, this is the craziest world, I told him no. I got in my car and started driving home. I sure get myself in the damest situations. I sure don't understand life. This isn't like the movies thats for sure. Wow, no one would ever believe this. Wow.

Chapter Fifteen

Joan, my water skiing
friend and a girl named
Connie were living in
Martinez. They had a
nice little apartment.
Joan was working in a
drive-in restaurant.
She did not last very
long tho, because she
kept having accidents.
First she spilled a
tray of milk shakes in

a guys new car, then she ran into the swinging
door, that all the car hops used. She said she
had it all timed to the second when to go
through the door but something happened. When
she got put working inside, she gave away extra scoops of ice cream and filled the bags of
french frys to full, and let some people go
without paying, so she got fired.

I went over to see Joan and try and cheer
her up, she was feeling bad about getting fired.
Joan said she was going to make me a cup of coffee. Well, I took a big drink of Joan's coffee
and I thought I was going to die. She accident-
ly put chile powder in the cup instead of what
she thought was instant coffee.

"Please don't be mad, honest it was a accident."

"Oh Joan, if it was anyone else I'd swear
they did it on purpose."

"Sharon I want you to meet some real life
beat nicks who live down stairs o.k?"

"O.k."

We went down stairs and Joan introduced me
to two guys and two girls. We sat down and
started drinking some wine. One girl stayed in
the bedroom and these two guys kept going in
and out of there. Joan told them I had a swimming pool where I lived so they ask me if they

121

could go swimming. We weren't supose to swim
after ten O'clock but I thought it would probably be o.k. just that once.

We drove over to my apartment. Joan didn't
come because she was still feeling bad about
losing her job. The swimming pool was in the
middle of two, two story apartment buildings.
All the apartments faced the swimming pool and
anyone swimming could clearly be seen. Well, we
got to the pool and all of a sudden the two
guys and the two girls started striping.

"What are you guys doing?"

"We're going swimming!"

I didn't know what to do, the four of them
were naked jumping in and out of the water
laughing and having a great time. The noise
echoed through the buildings and people started comming to look to see what was happening.

"Please, pretty please! Hey would you guys
put on your cloths."

"We can't we're all wet."

"Oh hell, come on in the apartment and I'll
get you some towels."

Jan met me and four naked people at the
door.

"Sharon! What in the hells going on?"

"A-well-a, I'll tell ya tomarrow, go back
to sleep."

"How can I go to sleep with four naked strangers in my apartment. What are you going to do
have some kind of orge?"

"They just went for a swim."

"A swim! What do you want to do get us kicked out of here or arested?"

"I'll just give them a towel and then they
will get dressed and I'll take them home o.k?"

"Sharon your a ass hole. If you ever do--oh
good night."

I took the four of them home and I can't
especially say I was sorry I never saw much of
them after that. Jan never let me forget about
that for days and every time someone knocked at

122

the door for a week, she thought it was about the four naked strangers.

My sister Kerry wanted me to take her out to a bar, she thought it would be exciting. So she and I went to this straight bar in Concord. It was supose to be a pretty nice place. We were sitting at the bar when this guy I went to school with came in. I hoped he didn't see us because I sure didn't want my sister to get to know him. Well, he saw us and came over to where we were sitting.

"Hi Sharon, how have you been?"

"O.k."

"Who is this lovely flower sitting next to you?"

"My sister."

Kerry looked up at him with blinking eyes and I wanted to hit her over the head with something.

"My names Bill and I haven't seen such beauty as yours in this establishment before."

"Thank you, my name is Kerry."

"It would be my pleasure to have the privilege of having just one dance with you."

"O.k."

"If you will excuse us Sharon."

"I ought to excuse you in the mouth."

"Sharon! He might hear you."

"So."

Oh brother did she fall for that line of junk. She walked away with him and had this shy dreamy look in her eyes. The rest of the night my little sister was swung and romanced around the dance floor. She was so cute and in her own sweet dream world of happiness. Her hero was the number one con artist in high school.

I still feel it was my fault for taking her in that dam bar. I should have my butt kicked for ever doing that. With in a few months I was a brides maid, in slacks, at Kerry and Bills wedding. I don't think my slacks were very popular, the wedding was in Bills mom and dads

123

house and I was the only one in our family
that knew about the wedding. Kerry begged me
not to tell mom and dad because there would
only be trouble and she was going to get married and no one was going to stop her. I could-
n't talk her out of it. Kerry was so innocent
and so sweet standing there with her big blue
eyes shinning. She was a little girl in love
and about to be carried away by a salesman con
artist, that I fought with all through school.
She said she really loved him, I truely hoped
it would work out and they would be happy.

I was playing softball for Pittsburg but I
wasn't doing very good. I also couldn't seem
to talk to any of the girls. It really frightened me to play ball in front of all those
people and it was getting worse not better. The
coach was getting mad at me and was losing what
little faith she had in me. We won the state
championship and the town of Pittsburg treated
us like real heros. Every time I was in Pittsburg someone would always say,

"You play ball don't you? We never miss a
game."
Charmaine got descharged from the service and
her grandmother wanted to send her to an unwed mothers home, that way no one would ever
know about her being pregnant. A girl couldn't
go through life with that hanging over her
head and she had to think of the rest of the
family. Charmaine was sent to Oakland and she
wrote me and told me where she was. She spent
a lot of time alone and did not get very many
visitors. I went over to see her every chance
I got and I also wrote to her. She said all the
babies were given away to lawyers and doctors.
She said long before you had your child, you
signed papers giving them up. She said she
could hear the girls screaming as they gave
birth to their babies. Charmaine said she was
scared. The girls that were in the home were
from 13 to 25 and they were given lessons on

self protection against pregnancy and on clean-
liness. When I'd go to see Charmaine we would
go down to a drive-in restaurant and buy milk
shakes for all the girls and sneak them in the
back door of the home. They were all on diets
and weren't supose to have milk shakes. They
would all be waiting for us at the back door.
They looked like a bunch of little kids and
soon as they got there milk shakes, they went
giggling off to there rooms with there treas-
ures. There was a awful saddness about that
place, a morning depressing atmosphere. On
Christmas I went to see Charmaine, she didn't
have any other visitors. When I got there she
had a present for me. A beautiful red knited
sweater, it was the nicest present anyone ever
give me. I had a present for her too, but it
wasn't very much. When I left her there I felt
very bad, I couldn't stand to see people I
cared about hurt. I didn't like to see anyone
hurt.

Charmaine had her baby and when she saw it,
she knew she couldn't give it away. So she
stole her baby and ran. When she showed up in
town with the baby everyone was shocked and
her secret was out in the open. Her friends
did not want to get involved and she explained
to me,

"You know how people make over a new baby?
Well, everyone just looked at my baby and acted real funny."

The adoption agency found her and they had
the papers to take the baby.

I will never forget the next time I saw
Charmaine. We were sitting in a restaurant having a coke and she was so tore up inside.

"Sharon you should have seen my baby it was
the most beautiful baby you ever saw. The tiny
little baby, do you think it will have a good
home, I wonder what they will teach it. Every
baby I see on the street remindes me of mine,
Oh god, I'm going to go around the rest of my

125

life not knowing if maybe I'll see my own child and not know it."

Charmaine got an apartment with two other girls from the unwed mothers home. It was in San Francisco. She got a job as a secreatary and some how life went on. She was a living breathing part of the city of tall lifeless buildings and hard paved streets and flashing lights but her eyes kept scearching every babies face and listening to every crying child knowing she could never find what she had lost.

My mother called me and told me my grandpa Smith was dead, my mom's dad. I took a weeks vacation, so I could go with my mom and brother Jim to my grandpa's funeral in Wyoming. All the way to Wyoming my mom just kept talking about my grandpa and all the things he said and the last time she saw him alive. The family tried to get grandpa to live in California but he loved Wyoming. I thought about the times I saw him. I only saw him about four times in my life, when he would come for about a week at a time to stay with us. Him and my grandma was devorced before I was born. He told me that he loved grandma and he never loved anyone else, but she wanted to live in California and he lived his whole life in Wyoming and could never leave it. I remember when he told me about this guy that tryed to ambush him when he was riding to town on his horse. He ran away from home when he was about thirteen and lived with the hole in the wall gang, that was really true too. After years of hard work he had his own ranch and had eight kids. Some how the ranch caught on fire and he lost everything.

The last time I saw my grandpa he gave me a dollar. I told him I didn't want it but he said it would hurt his feelings if I didn't take it. He lived on an old age pension and I knew when he gave me that dollar it was more than just a dollar and he couldn't aford to give it to me. He was ninty four years old but

126

he had a mind that was as clear and sharp as a young person. He was 6 ft. 4 inches, and slightly bent with age. His hair was silver and his eyes were always laughing and I never heard him say a bad thing about anyone.

The county was going to bury my grandpa, but he was too tall to fit in the county casket, so they were going to break his back so they could fit him in it. All of us got there in time to stop it and my mom and aunts payed for his funeral. We went up to the little room he lived in. He had his Christmas cards hung on his kitchen cabinets and walls. The letter I had written him was laying opened on his dresser. His room wasn't very neat but he was half blind and deaf so I guess he must of been quite a person to be able to take care of his self and never ask anyone for anything. That beautiful old man with all his love and humaneness died alone.

Grandpa said he wanted everyone to get drunk and have a good time when he died. We all went into the little bar he lived over and ordered some drinks. The bar tender wouldn't let us pay for the drinks. He loved the old man that use to come in there and play cards. That day at the funeral was the first time I ever saw my mother cry. She looked like a frightened little bird caught in a rain storm, and the rain would not quit falling. I never seen anything so heart breaking in my life.

Joan was going with this guy and when they broke up he went over to her mothers house with a list of everything he had bought for her when he took her out. Right down to every coke. He told Joans mom that he expected to get every cent back, she said she never heard of such a thing. He sure was mad when he couldn't get his money back.

Jan introduced me to a girl named Bonnie, she met through a girl on the ball team. Bonnie was going to college and lived with her

grandparents in a big fancy house in Laffette.
I didn't like going around with anyone that
came from a rich family but she didn't act
like a snob. Her grandma was a real nice person and she liked me and treated me very nice.
Bonnie was a very sexy pretty girl and she had
a I.Q. of a hundred and thirty something. She
couldn't stand the way I talked and started
telling me all this stuff about, I saw, instead of I seen. Everyone I knew said I seen
and it about drove me crazy trying to stop saying it when no one said I saw. I really wanted
to make love to her but every time we were just
about to, something would happen. Someone was
always at the apartment. One day we went over
to my mom and dads, I had to change the oil in
my car and use my dad's grease gun to grease
it. Anyway she was sitting on the couch and no
one was home so we started making out and I
started touching her and we were both getting
upset and my mom and dad pulled up in the
drive way. Oh well, you can't have everything.

We had a big party at work and had drinks
and everyone was getting drunk. My boss was
really something. He was having an affair with
one woman there and at the party him and another woman were in the back room. Everyone
was danceing and getting drunk. One of the
girls and I got to talking and big mouth me
told her I was gay. She ask me if I had ever
been to bed with a guy and said I couldn't say
I was gay until I went to bed with a guy and
seen if I liked it.

When I came back to work the next day everyone acted real funny. The girl had told everyone. It was awful the way everyone changed
and it really hurt me. I'll never forget the
look in this one womans face as she talked to
me. She acted like I was some awful creature
or something and before she was so nice and
liked me. I didn't know what to think or do.
Bonnie wanted me to go with her to her parents

ranch, for a couple of weeks. So after working there a year, I quit my job and went with
Bonnie to her parents ranch.

Bonnie's mom and step dad were really rich.
I couldn't hardly believe it. They had this
big house in Fresno, with a swimming pool and
a gardener. Then they had this great big ranch
with a forman and cows and horses and Bonnie
had a little colt. Bonnie got me so confused
telling me all this correct english to talk I
couldn't remember which word was right and
which one was wrong. I just decided not to say
anything except yes and no. Her mom and step
dad were very nice. We had dinner in the living
room by the fire place. Her parents ate in the
dinning room. The living room was decorated
western stile and that fire place was beautiful. They had these special logs that burned
blue flames and sparkled star shaped sparks.
We would sit by the fire place and make out
when we were alone. The room was a soft red
and her eyes danced with the fire light and
her soft body was close to mine. We would take
walks in the hills and she would chace me and
then I would chace her. We laughed and played
and never seemed to get tired. Our favorite
place was by this water fall that spilled mountain water into a deep blue pool. I helped her
up the side of the water fall, she was so fem
sometimes and I just loved it. She had been
with quite a few women and she knew a lot about
sex. She said she was in love with this woman
in Laffette. We were having an affair.

The hours of love making were passionate,
warm and thrilling. I learned about the real
sweetness and feelings of every part of the
body and we walked in the moon light and were
lovers for a time.

Chapter Sixteen

I went down and put in
for my unemployment
benefits, I got a five
week penalty because I
quit my job. Janice got
fired and got a five
week penalty, so I don't
think it mattered what
you did you still got a
five week penalty. Af-
ter five weeks, I would
get $28.00 a week unem-
ployment. I started looking for another job and
it was the shits. I had to get all dressed up
in a dress and high heels, which I hated and
then go into all these places and fill out papers by the dozens. The thing that bothered me
the most was the way people treated you. When
you went in the offices, they looked you up
and down. The offices were as quiet as a church,
and it made you afraid to breath. They had a
way of talking to you that made you feel like
you were beging for a crust of bread or something.

"We're not hiring!"

"Why did you quit your last job?"

Oh everyone found out I was a queer and I
couldn't take it. Oh sure I was going to say
that. I had to write something so I put that I
quit because I had to take care of my sick
grandmother. Well that's all I could think of.

"Fill out an application and we'll call you
if we have an opening."

"Don't call us, we'll call you," I thought.

I was living at home and my dad was back on
the kick of me going to bed at nine o'clock. He
said I was lazy and didn't have any ambition
and even if I could get a job, I probably would-
n't get out of bed. It made him sick to look at
me and I was probably going to end up in the

gutter or washing dishes somewhere.

Jan was going with Connie and Joan was staying with them. They had an apartment in San Francisco. I decided to go over there to look for a job. My dad said I couldn't go, would you believe I was twenty, oh well, I got in the car and left anyway. I put in about a hundred more applications and between times Jan and I played checkers and monopoly and drank beer. This one day I came in from looking for a job and Jan wanted to take a picture of me in my dress. I got this red mop wig Jan had and put it on and she took the picture. Joan was going to the bath room and Jan took a picture of her. She was really mad and we laughed and laughed.

We went to this new bar in San Francisco to see a drag show. That was the first time I ever saw a drag show. These guys got up and impersonated women. They were beautiful and wore these fine gowns that looked very expensive. They moved just like women and they had good figures and most of them had pretty faces. They looked like those upper class women in the movies. They did impersonations of famous women and flerted with all the guys and the butches. This one guy came out in a two peace bathing suit and his body didn't look anything like a guys and he pulled off this top at the end of the number and through his false's to the audience. This other guy showed his private part and it was a woman's private part. I ask Jan how he could do that?

"He has a artificial thing on that just makes him look that way."

"Oh."

This woman came in the bar and sat next to me and we started talking. She seemed very nice and she told me she had been married and it didn't work out. She had a very good job and she was thirty years old. She dressed very nice and she was pretty and we danced and she kept flerting with me. She was sure a woman

131

and when she rubbed herself on me it really upset me. She went to the bath room and Jan came
over and started talking to me.
   "You going to take her to bed?"
   "Sh-I don't know, I don't even know her."
   "You said you were horney, didn't you?"
   "Well-a-ya."
   "Well go to bed with her."
   That Jan was to much, sitting there saying
all that but I ended up going home with the
woman. She took me up on this hill to look at
a veiw of San Francisco, and we started making
out and then went to her apartment. Wow, it
was getting to be really something. I sure was
in and out of a lot of bedrooms. Every woman
was different too. She was so open and she just
came to me so fine. I made love to her all
night and neither one of us wanted to stop. She
kept wispering to me and her body responded to
my every touch and I felt like I couldn't do
anything wrong. She run her hands over my back
and through my hair and she kept pulling me
closer and closer. She fit next to me so nice
and her body was so warm and we swam in the
warmth and feelings of each other. It was morning and I had to go and she didn't want me to
leave her. I told her I would see her the following week end and she gave me her phone number. We stood in the door way kissing and I
didn't want to go but I had to. I drove over
to Jan's to say good by to them before I went
home.
   "Sharon, was she any good?"
   "Oh shit Jan, your to much, she was real
nice o.k."
   "Nice, was she any good in bed?"
   "Ya, ya, she was."
   When I got home my dad was really mad. He
said he was going to sell my car, because I
didn't do what he told me to and went to San
Francisco.
   "I payed for that car with my money."

"It's in my name, so I'm going to sell it."

He took the car to a car lot and left it there. He found out he couldn't get very much money for it and my mom talked him out of selling it. He sat in his chair in the living room and started telling me how stupid I was and that I would never find another job and that I was no good.

"Go to hell."

He got up and started sluging me and I took my foot and kicked him and he stumbled back and then caught his ballance and came at me again. Then my sister Kerry started screaming and my mom told him to stop. I looked at him and yelled. "Your crazy." He stood there with this funny look on his face and then he said, "I know it."

He stood there and tears were rolling down his cheeks and his eyes looked so lost. I hated myself for doing that to my father. I wished I was dead, all I ever did was hurt people, or let them down. I told him I was sorry, I was really sorry but the words didn't take away what had happened. I would see him standing there like that for the rest of my life.

The coach called me and said she wanted to talk to me. I went over there and she said she was going to lone me to another team. She said I could still go on all the trips with them and all the girls liked me very much but it would be better for me to play for this other team. I did not blame her for not believing in me but I felt sick inside and very hurt. I felt like just giving up playing ball all together.

I went to the first practice and was going to tell my new coach, Lilly, I was going to quit. When I got to talk to her she said she wanted me to be their catcher and the whole team was very glad I was playing for them. She said they thought I was a very good ball player. Lilly started practice and for the first time in my life I was playing catcher. It was hard

133

getting use to the batter swinging the bat right
next to my head and keeping from blinking, so
you could catch the ball when there was a strike.
Lilly wanted this girl named Carol to pitch and
so she and I started practicing together a lot.
She didn't want to pitch and was having a hard
time. I talked to her and told her she could be
a very good pitcher. She and I started practicing together all the time and we became very
close. She said she didn't think she could pitch
unless I caught.

Our team started developing and we were all
very close and stuck together. It was a wonderful feeling hearing the croud cheering us on
and working together. Even when we lost we still
were happy just being a team and playing ball
and I thought that was more important than anything. Every ball game was exciting and everyone yelled and encourged each other.

"No batter in there, Carol."

"Chuck that ball in there to Sharon."

"Right over, strike three."

"Way to go."

Game after game we stuck together and I
wasn't scared anymore. We were having a practice before a big game and Margaret was running into home and I taged her and hurt my hand.

"Oh shit."

"Is it very bad?"

"Let me see."

"Sharon we're going to have to take you to
the hospital, I think it is broken."

"What are we going to do?"

Well I had a broken hand, so the team had
to find another catcher. Carol's mom was so
nice she said the team couldn't win with out
me and she was really worried about my hand.
Carol was so sweet she kept calling me and said
I had to go to the ball games to give them suport and cheer them on. I was beginning to really
care about Carol and I didn't want to because
she was to young. Jan came back from San Fran-

134

cisco and started playing third base. Her and
Connie had broken up and Connie and Joan were
staying in San Francisco.

Carol told me she knew about being gay and
she told me about the people she knew that were
gay. She kept asking me questions about it. We
went swimming and sat on the beech and looked
into each others eyes and just enjoyed being
together without any words. On the way back from
the beech I didn't see this stop sign and a
truck was speeding and run into us. My car was
totaled out but we weren't hurt. I was thrown
against the steering wheel and broke it. I did-
n't want to go home, my dad was going to kill
me.

My dad cussed and yelled and called me a
bunch of names. I got two hundred dollars for
my car, from the insurence company. It was
worth about eight hundred. I decided to buy a
honda 50, I never seen a girl ride a motar
cycle but I got one anyway. I really felt like
everything was going wrong and I was getting
awful tired. This woman Bo, that lived around
the corner from our house and who use to live
by my sister Billie, told me she wanted me to
come over and talk to her. She was very understanding and kept wanting me to come over. She
was married and had two boys. I kept thinking
she would find out I was gay and tell my mom.
The more I got to know her I relized she was
a pretty wonderful person and she would never
tell my mom anything. She was very interested
in everything I did and if I didn't know she
was straight I would have thought she liked me.
I told Jan about it and she said she thought
that Bo was interested in me. I told her I
thought she was wrong.

Jan and I rode my honda to practice and
while we were waiting to start she wanted
to ride it around.

"Jan I can't let you."
"Some friend you are."

135

"It hasn't anything to do with friendship."
"Let her ride it Sharon."
"Oh shit, go ahead."
Well she got on it, then Carol came up and
got on the back with her. I tried to stop them
but they took off and it looked like they just
headed for the nearest poll and that was it my
honda was recked. Nom had a station wagon and
so we put the bike in it and they took me home.
My mom and dad were staying in Redding, my dad
had a job there. I was sure glad of that. Jan
and Carol were very sorry but neither of them
had any money to get my bike fixed. They left
and I walked down to the store and got two six
packs of beer.

I sat there drinking one beer after another.
What in the hell was I going to do. Did I even
want to do anything? My little dog champ kept
looking at me like he knew everything I was
thinking. I couldn't take any more and all I
did was hurt people and mess up when they believed in me. I walked in the kitchen and took
a bottle of pills. Then I sat down and it was
really strange sitting there waiting to die.
Waiting for the unknown. I saw this movie once
and in it this person committed suicide and it
showed them in the inferno's of hell, falling
in this pit of fire. I thought a pit of fire
would probably be better than the living hell
I was going through. I called Carol and told
her I thought she should get married and have
fifteen kids. She ask me what was wrong and I
said nothing and hung up.

I couldn't stand the waiting so I went in
the bath room and got a razor blade. I couldn't
stand the sight of blood so I took it and cut
about five good cuts across my wrist in several
different directions to make sure I cut a vain.
I dropped my hand to my side, I couldn't look
at it. I felt my strenth draining out of me.
It was really weird, I could feel my life leaving my body. Champ was crying and howling, he
136

knew what was happening. I got another beer and sat down, my head felt so light and everything was so strange. I was going to die alone, I started crying. Blood was all over and it was only going to be a few minutes. No one could stop it. I could take Bo a beer and then I wouldn't die alone. I couldn't hardly walk. I felt so weak but I got to Bo's house and she sat me down and I wouldn't let them take me to the hospital. She called the hospital and they carried me to the car. I was talking crazy and didn't understand anything.

They got me to the hospital and rushed me in and sewed up my arm and pumped out my stomack. I had twenty one stiches in my arm, they gave me a fifty, fifty chance to live. They put me in a paded cell in the psychiatric ward. The next day my brother Jim came in to see me.

"Dam you Sharon. Why did you pull a trick like this, if anything happens to mom and dad, its all your fault. I fixed it where this won't go on your record, or you won't go to jail. I cleaned up the mess you made at the house, all those beer cans and blood. I hope you didn't wreck mom and dads rug. I got to go, don't you ever do anything like this again."

I couldn't even die right. My mom and dad came to see me and my dad just sat there crying and looking a thousand years old and my mom just sat there with this emty look on her face. Why do I always end up hurting everyone? Oh I wish I could just have never been born. They said I could never be left alone again and they wouldn't hardly let me out of there sight.

Chapter Seventeen

I couldn't leave the
hospital until I saw
the psychiatrist and he
released me. I walked
in his office and the
first thing he ask me
was, "What did you do,
get in a fight with
your girl friend?"
"What makes you think
I got a girl friend?"
"I'm going to release
you and I want you to understand that you can
get psychiatric help here at the hospital. Is
there anything you want to talk about before
you go?"

"No."

"O.k. you can go."

Maybe I was crazy. I sure was ending up in
a lot of psychiatrists offices. Jan said that
the girls on the first team I played for found
out about me trying to kill myself and said
they thought I was a mixed up kid. She said
when they found out about that they really lost
there faith in me. Well, what was I going to
do? I didn't want anyone to believe in me, because there was something in me that just wasn't
any good and it sure was a mistake when I didn't
die.

Bo came over to see me and she said that I
had insisted that she stay in the room with me
when they were sewing me up and everything. She
said she held my hand through the whole thing.
Bo was really nice and she talked to me and I
felt she understood. There was something very
warm about her. She wasn't pretty or fem on
the outside but she seemed to have all her beauty on the inside. She thought and looked at
things in a way that made everything seem alright. I was beginning to like her more every

time I saw her.

Carol and Jan were seeing a lot of each other and I knew Carol was falling for Jan. I couldn't blame Carol because I could remember how I felt about Jan and how she made me feel. I didn't have a chance with Carol and besides I didn't ever want to mess around with a seventeen year old kid. Well, it seemed no matter what I thought or felt I wasn't very lucky in love any way.

I was riding my bike around the block and was turning a corner in second gear very slowly and my bike slid in some gravel and down I went. I thought I just skinned my knee and I was worried about my bike being messed up. The corner was by Bo's house and she was standing outside. I went over to talk to her and she ask me if I was o.k. I said yes and was looking at my bike and it was o.k.

"Sharon look at your knee, it's really bad!"

Well, Bo took me to the hospital again and all I could think of was, my mom and dad were really going to be mad and I would probably never get to ride my bike again. My knee was a mess it was all crushed and had a big hole in it. The doctor cleaned it out and said he couldn't sew much together because it was such a mess. The flesh was all tourn and the bone was showing. He could only get three stiches in it and gave me some stuff to put on it. My leg was stiff and my mom and dad were decusted in me and I was decusted in me too.

My dad had to go back to Redding to work and I had to go to. I couldn't be left alone because I might try and kill myself again. Redding is really something, the temperature was about 120. We were staying in this little town outside of Redding, called Cottonwood. My sister Billie's husband, Chester was working with my dad on the construction job. Billie and the kids had to stay in Pittsburg.

Dad was the best heavy equipment operator

139

they had and they usually gave him all of the
hardest jobs. He never missed a day of work
and was never late and he worked very hard.
Dad was fifty nine and his life of hard work
was beginning to show. His hands were one sol-
id calluse and he had to wear a suport for his
back. The foreman of the company was giving
dad a bad time and adding to everything else.
Mom and dad were worried about dad lasting until he could retire.

Even when you were in the house, you could
hardly stand the heat. The guys on the construction crew took salt tablets and wore hats but
the sun beat down on them with its giant fists.
Chester had to work inside of the trench they
were digging. This one day after he had been
in the trench for quite a while, dad stoped the
machine he was running and went to see what
happened to Chester. Chester had passed out in
the trench and was just lieing there. They pulled him out of the trench and then everyone went
to the nearest bar for a beer and the next day
they were all back to work.

Dad had worked on jobs, on the sides of
mountains and he had set dinamight and did just
about every dirty job the company had ever ask
him to do and more. Chester also worked and
gave everything he had for a construction company that had no feelings for the lives or the
sweat and blood that a few strong backed men
spent there lives giving out on hot dirty back
roads.

My mom and dad loved to go fishing and so
every weekend we all went fishing. That was a
great place to fish and we caught our limit almost every time we went fishing. My leg was
getting better but it was still stiff. I had
my bike and I started riding it and I bent my
leg enough to ride the bike but it wasn't easy.
I rode back in the hills and found this pretty
lake and looked at the sky so big and full of
soft clouds. I was very lonely and I got a

letter from Jan and she told me about all the
things her and Carol were doing. I had all
these feelings inside me, I didn't know what
they were and my mind couldn't sort them out.
All I knew was Carol and Jan were together.

Bo sent me these two letters and they were
beautiful. I couldn't believe she was real.
The depth and warmth and feelings were so fine,
I never met a woman like her before. I kept
reading the letters over and over, she had the
most beautiful insides I ever seen. That was
the most important thing in the world to be
beautiful inside, because your insides is the
real you and thats the part that a person has
to know and love.

I got home and Bo came over and invited me
to dinner. We talked for hours and she told me
she knew I was gay. She said she had been in
love with this girl before she was married and
the girl had died. She said I remined her of
that girl. That was really something to love
someone and then for them to die. I thought
that was the deepest of heart breaks. She was a
fine person and she always smiled and looked at
the world in such a cheerful understanding way.
Her husband Mike seemed to be a nice guy. He
had a job working for the state and he was home
only on weekends. They invited me to go everywhere with them.

I didn't know much about kids because I
never was around them much. Nickie, Bo's young-
est boy, was two. No one liked him and he just
ran around crying all the time. He was his dads
favorite and Mike just packed him around all
the time when he was home. All the kid would
eat was fryed eggs and no one could do anything
with him. This one night we were comming back
from going swimming and Nickie was laying in
the front seat asleep. His face was all dirty
and he was a mess. He looked like a poor lost
little kid that no one loved. I decided right
then, I was going to be friends with him and

some how, I thought I knew how he felt.

Rickie was a smart little kid and he was eight. He acted like a little old lady and had a vocabulary better than most grown ups I knew. He showed me his bug collection and I talked Bo into letting him keep his bugs in the house. He told me all about his school and showed me his grades and they were really good. He was really a nice kid. Rickie was not Mikes son but Mike adopted him. Bo had Rickie before she married Mike. Bo didn't think Mike treated Rickie right and Rickie felt his dad didn't either. Rickie didn't know he was adopted and Mike wasn't his real father.

Bo's dad and brother lived with them also. Her dad had a nick name Mr. Smith. He wanted to be called Mr. Smith because everyone always said his name wrong. He was a jolly old man and he looked kind of like santa and he was always joking and laughing. Mr. Smith really liked me and him and I would sit and talk and drink coffee. He was a very famious man and he would tell me about when he was a cameraman for Fox studios and worked in Hollywood. He was a photographer and he worked his way through college and his professors wanted him to be a surgeon. He had his own photography studio in Concord. He took pictures for the government and he had taken the last pictures of Amealia Airheart before she disapeared. He also took the first pictures of the Port Chicago explosion. He lost his studio and almost everything he had. He and his wife and children moved to the project in Pittsburg. He would sit and tell me about the past and laugh and joke. He was really a wonderful old man.

Bo's mother died about a year and a half before. She had been a concert violinist and had traveled and studied in Europe, she also studied to be a nun. Everyone loved her and thought she was one of the greatest women they knew. She died of cancer and layed and suffered

for a year before she died. Mr. Smith always
talked about her with this sad far away look
in his eyes and talked about how much he missed her. Paul, Bo's brother couldn't read hardly
at all and she said it happened after their mother died. Paul was fifteen and there was something very sad about him, he would laugh and
talk but deep down inside he was very unhappy
and lonely.

I started spending most of my time over at
Bo's and everyone was so nice. We would all
sit out in the front yard under this tree and
talk and drink beer. All the neighbors would
come over and we would laugh and have a great
time. The lady that lived next door to Bo was
going to have a baby. Her husband came home
one night drunk and she was having some pains
so he said she was having the baby and he was
going to deliver it. He rubbed lard all over
his hands and started trying to pull her baby
out of her. He almost killed her and the baby
before the kids could get the neighbors to
stop him.

Bo and I drove over to her sister Dee's
house. When we got there the place was full of
cops. Dee's boy friend Banks had spit in the
lady next doors face so her two sons had worked him over with a hammar. Banks and Dee came
over to the car and Banks had blood all over
him.

"Banks get in and we'll take you to the
hospital."

"I ain't goin to no mother fucken hospital.
I'm gonna go out and find those mother fuckers
and kill them."

"You can sign a complaint against them."

"I ain't signin nothin, I'm gonna kill them."

Well, I was glad when we left and I do think
that was something else. Banks was one mean
mother and he was always into something. The
next time I saw him and Dee he was real quiet
and nice and didn't even seem like the same

143

guy. That was the way Banks was and he had
everyone scared of him and he could really
pull some stuff and get away with it. He beat
Dee up real bad and she came over to stay with
Bo because she was afraid he was going to kill
her. Both Dee's eyes were black and her face
was all messed up. She really looked awful.

My mom and dad didn't like Bo and wanted
me to quit going over to her house. I didn't
want to stop going over there. They were all
so nice to me and liked me and I liked them
too.

We were sitting in Bo's living room talking and it was about one o'clock and everyone
was asleep. I stood up to leave and Bo came
over to me and was standing so close to me and
was looking at me. I couldn't help it I kissed her and we went into the bedroom and I took
her cloths off and started making love to her.
I kept thinking I must be out of my mind, there
I was making love to a married woman, in a
whole house full of people.

The next night we got on my bike and rode
up in the hills and there on a hill under the
stars I made love to her again. She filled me
with warmth and she came to me wholly and I
knew she loved me. She was so open and giving
and her soft sweetness made explosions inside
of me and we came together and held each other
in the deepest moments of my life. We layed
there looking at the stars and feeling each
others warmth and knew we couldn't stand to
be apart again. Words couldn't express what we
felt and we looked at each other and knew how
it was. Her arms were around me as we rode
under a sky filled with stars and the wind was
soft and gentle. I drove slow because I didn't
want her to leave me, even if just for a night.

When we got back to my house Jan and Carol
was there and they said Mike was looking for
Bo and he was really mad. They said they were
leaving because they didn't want to get invol-
144

ved. Bo and I went over to her house and Mike came out the door screaming.

"I'm going to rap that bike around your neck Sharon."

"Just try it."

Bo started talking to Mike and told me to go home. I didn't want to leave her with him so mad. She said she could take care of everything and so I went home. She called me the next morning and told me to come over for coffee and Mike was real nice. She was a real good talker.

Mike left for the week and then I started staying there until day light every morning and then going home before my mom and dad woke up. It was really something sneeking around like that always worried about getting caught. I couldn't keep away from her and when Mike was home on the weekends I thought I would go nuts. I loved her but she was married and I didn't want to break up someones marriage. She told me her marriage was over before she met me and she didn't love Mike, she loved me and she was going to get a devorce.

Chapter Eighteen

I felt like a leaf
caught in the middle
of a storm, everything
was happening so fast
and all I could do was
silently stand by. Bo
and Dee figured out
how Bo could get a de-
vorce and they planned,
how Bo would tell Mike.
Bo, talked to Mike and
they went over every-
thing and she was very kind to him. He seemed
o.k. until he came to get his cloths. He started yelling and cussing and Bo told him to leave.
Then he stood out in front of their house screaming at the top of his lungs, that we were two
queers.

"You dirty bitchs! Go ahead and sit around
and suck each other off, I don't give a fuck!
I'm going to fight you mother fuckers in court!
You dirty cock suckers! You lousy god dam
queers!"

Then he went around to all the neighbors
and told them about how I broke up their marriage and turned his wife queer. Then he went
to everyone in Bo's family and to every friend
they had and told them too. Everyone in Martinez, Pittsburg and Concord knew about us,
after Mike got through. He said he was going
to go over and tell my parents. I told him to
go ahead and my dad would punch him in the
mouth. He didn't go over there but they still
heard about everything.

We would get in the car to go somewhere and
everyone would stare at us like we were some
kind of weird freaks or something. My mom and
dad begged me not to go over to Bo's house any
more and my mom said,

"Sharon everyone is saying you broke up Bo
146

and Mikes marriage."

It was really awful, it was like everyone
in the world was against us. We knew we had to
move away from the neighborhood. I sold my bike
and got a $100.00 dollars for it and we rented
a two story house in Martinez. Dee rented the
bottom part of the house and we rented the top
part.

My mother begged me not to move in with Bo
and said she hated Bo. She cryed when I left
and said, "I wasn't any daughter of hers." I
made my mother cry, I felt like a dirty D.O.B.
and my dad said he knew I wasn't any good.
Wow, I really did it this time.

Mike said he was going to take the kids
away from Bo and name me as corespondent, in
their devorce. He tried to take Rickie out of
school but Rickie wouldn't go with him. Mike
came over to our house and him and Bo talked
and talked. She was a good talker and so he
quit being so violent but he came over to the
house almost every weekend. He told Dee, he
was going to get Bo in bed and get her pregnant then she couldn't devorce him. Bo would-
n't go to bed with him and finally he quit
comming over so often.

It seemed in those days like nothing was
on our side and we just kept having a lot of
trouble. We didn't have enough money to live
on and I was having a hard time finding a job.
There were days when Bo and I went without
anything to eat but we always had something
for Rickie and Nickie. The only thing that
kept us from giving up or going nuts, was the
strength of our feelings and when the four of
us were together nothing else mattered. We
lived by a little park and we would take walks
in the park and I made Rickie a sling-shot and
showed him how to shoot a bebe gun. His eyes
would shine and he would smile and we all laughed. Nickie, followed me everywhere and I started teaching him how to talk. He couldn't talk

147

at all, he could only say about three words.
They were really wonderful kids, any thing we
did was fun. Bo had the most beautiful smile
I ever saw and a way of looking at me, that
just made me warm all over. I think those days
and walks were a wonderful deep part of my
life I never want to forget. We would go to
the drive-in on $1.00 night and invite Dee and
her little girl and Mr. Smith and Paul. Everyone would bring something and we always had a
good time.

We decided to call our house the sugar shack
after this popular song. Me and Rickie made
this sign and put it on our door. The house was
a old ugly looking two story house that sat on
a hill away from the new apartment buildings,
that were being built. The land lord said they
were going to tear it down in about a year.
Everyone that came to the sugar shack said the
minute you walked in the door you could feel
the love and warmth. I never heard people say
that before and I was very proud because love
in a home is the most important thing in the
world. Everyone started comming over to our
house and some were straight and some were gay
and we would laugh and play games or just talk.
I never felt such a sence of belonging and
friendship and love in my life. Everyone was
welcome at the sugar shack and we never locked
our doors or turned anyone away. Some people
laughed at us, some called us names and some
even thought we were running a house of prostitutes but we had a lot of friends and love.

I got a job in a convalescent hospital.
They could only give me three hours a day as
a dish washer for $1.25 a hour. Bo talked to
a lawyer and got $100.00 a month child suport.
My first check I bought Rickie some school
cloths, he was going to school with patches in
his pants and the kids were teasing him. He
was a very sensitive little kid and very shy.
The kids were pushing him around at school, so

148

I started teaching him how to defend himself.
Some times you have to fight.

I'll never forget our first Christmas, we
didn't have any money so we took our rent money and spent it on toys. Bo was such a good
talker, she told the land lord that we would
pay him the next month and he was real nice.
We decided to buy a lot of small presents instead of just a couple big ones because that
way the kids wouldn't think they weren't getting very much. We went to payless store in
Concord and got what looked like a whole lot
for what money we had. We had so much fun getting a tree and all of us decorating it and
Bo and I wraped the presents. I like to try
and wrap presents, so you couldn't guess what
they were. We got Rickie a football. It looked
like something from outer space and Rickie
said he was going to open it first because he
sure couldn't figure out what it was. I went
down to a store in Martinez where my mom and
dad had credit and talked them into giving me
credit. I bought Bo a ring and on Christmas
eve of 1963, I gave it to her. We made love
all night and I loved her so much and it just
kept getting stronger.

Rickie and Nickie were really happy with
there presents and we all played with the toys
and Rickie had me help him with his science
kits. Nickie was all smiles, he was so cute and
everyone said they couldn't believe he was the
same kid, he wasn't a brat any more. That really made me feel good because everyone liked
Nickie now and he didn't go around crying and
his face was still dirty but he was smiling
and his eyes were happy.

Mike and all his relations came over and
brought the kids some presents. I told Bo I
had to go over to my mom and dads for a while
and she got mad. My mom and dad were still mad
at me and all the rest of the family was too,
except Kerry and Billie. Kerry use to come to

visit Bo and I and Kerry gave us a present. I
felt so sorry for Kerry she was really having
a lot of trouble with her husband. He was always drinking and wouldn't work, I felt guilty
I shouldn't have ever taken her to that dam bar
where she met him. Everyone was at mom and dads
for Christmas dinner and were pretty nice to
me. Dad, Bob and Jim gave me a shot of wiskey,
we always drank straight shots of wiskey together on holidays. When I had to go they got mad
because I wouldn't have Christmas dinner with
them. I was single and my place was with my
parents on holidays and I should be living at
home any way and saving my money, instead of
living with some old woman with a bunch of
kids. Bo was twenty six and I was twenty one
you sure couldn't tell by the way my parents
talked. My mother wouldn't hardly talk to me
and she said she didn't want Bo's name men-
tioned in her house.

Carol and Nom and Jan came over. Carol and
Nom brought Bo and I a present. Mr. Smith and
Paul was there too, also Dee, Banks and Deniece.
Dee and Banks bought us a carton of cigarettes.
The house was full of laughter and we all put
our money together and had the best Christmas
dinner in the world. Mr. Smith ate more than
anyone and he didn't eat one piece of punkin
pie but a half of a punkin pie, he said,

"Don't hand me some little'o piece of pie,
just cut it down the middle and save the other
half for later."

We all cleaned up the kitchen and then we
started playing cards and laughing. I think
that was about the best Christmas any of us
ever had.

At work they put me on full time and I started working eight hours a day. I hated working
there but I couldn't quit until I found a better job. It was awful the way the cook just
barely gave those people enough food. Ever
chance I got I gave them extra food. The owner

of the place didn't hire enough people to do
all the work that had to be done so we really
had a lot of work to do. That convalescent hospital was filled with expensive furniture and
big chandeliers. It was all landscaped and fancy. The cook got a kick back for all the money
she could save on food. There wasn't enough
nurses aids, some of those old people died of
starvation and others layed in those expensive
beds with bed soars they got from not being
taken care of. I never got use to the way
those old people usually died in twos or threes
or sometimes fours or fives. Some of them ate
in this dinning room, the ones that could walk.
They got the best food because most of them
were mentally alert or had kids that were always checking on them. Even those old people
sat at their fancy tables with big flower ar-
rangements and seemed to have this cloud of
death hanging over there heads. There wasn't
very many smiles or laughter. Each face was
special and each a human being but they had
been handed the virdict and were being put to
death because of being old and not wanted and
they felt the emtyness and the non care. A
slow lonely death in a expensive way while the
smiling faces kissed there money and spoke
sweet lines of death.

On holidays people would come around and
sing Christmas carols and send little paper
things to put on the old peoples dinner plates.
This one old woman that looked like she should
have been taken care of, use to come around
once a week and sit with the old people and
show them how to make things. They liked that
and a lot of the time I could hear them laugh
or see them smile. When I went home sometimes
I just wanted to sit or maybe cry or something
but I couldn't and it was hard for me to explain my feelings or to stop thinking about
those old people. I wished I knew what to do
or what really hurt was the thought that no

one really cared, I didn't want to believe
that.

Rickie liked me to help him with his home
work and I liked helping him too. Nickie was
so cute, he would come running and jump in my
arms every night when I came home. Sometimes
he would hide and I would have to find him and
Bo and Rickie would say, "We don't know where
Nickie is, he just disappeared."

Then Nickie would jump up with a big grin
and say. "Here I am." Bo would always have my
bath water ready and fix dinner. I never had
anyone do things like that for me.

After dinner we would always talk or Banks
or Dee would come up to play cards and we
would make home made donuts or cookies and
laugh. Banks was a cook in the navy for about
eight years and he could really cook good. We
would have picnics at the park on my days off
and Banks and Dee would get part of the stuff
and we would get some beer and play baseball
or just sit around talking and laughing.

Banks and Dee were living together and Dee
said she loved him but he would go on these
drunks and get violent and she would kick him
out of the house. Everyone was afraid of Banks
because you never knew what he would do. I
wasn't afraid of him and he knew I wasn't. He
was scared and mixed up inside and he would
push people around and that made him feel better maybe he knew I knew. I don't know but
he never tried to push me around. This one day
Dee came up to our house and said he was going
to beat her up. I locked the door and went out
on the porch to wait for him. He came up and
I was ready for him and he knew it. He walked
around me, I just stood there, I never had
anyone walk around me before, it was like he
was saying this isn't our fight or something.
Before I knew it he had put his fist through
the window and he was yelling at Dee and he
was standing there with blood pouring out of

his wrist. A vain was cut and he was bleading
bad, he just stood there yelling.

"Banks come on I'm going to take you to the
hospital."

"I don't want to go to no fuckin hospital."

"Come on Banks, your going to blead to
death."

"I don't give a fuck."

Then he turned around and walked down the
stairs and I took him to the hospital. It was
a good thing too because the doctor said he
could have blead to death. He and I became
sort of friends but he was always saying us
men and I knew I wasn't no man and it bugged
me the way he was always saying that. Banks
and I worked on cars and rebuilt a engine for
Mr. Smiths car. One night Banks came home and
told us he had just been in a car with some
guys that shot a guy down and killed him in
Pittsburg. He went around for a week afraid of
his own shadow and the killing was in the news-
paper. He never got caught.

Dee and Banks ask us to baby sit for Denice,
so they could go out and have a few drinks.
They woke us up at three o'clock in the morning and they had cuts all over them. They had
been in a wreck and Dee said she didn't know
what they run into. They were both really drunk
and Dee was pregnant. Bo said she was taking
them to the hospital and Banks kept saying,

"I know it sounds crazy but I swear to god
I saw a jack ass. I saw this god dam big jack
ass come from nowhere, I swear I saw a jack
ass."

"Banks, I think your crazy, I never saw any
jack ass. Your drunk Banks and crazy too."

"I swear Dee, I thought I saw a jack ass."

Bo took them to the hospital and the doctor
took all kinds of glass out of them. The cops
found Banks car and it seemed that they had
run into a horse on the highway and when Banks
found out all he could say was,

"I knew I saw a jack ass, god dam it, I knew I wasn't crazy even if it was a horse."

Everything was calm for a while and we all laughed about the jack ass for a long time after that.

Bo wrote me some love poems and I wrote her some too. Wow her poems were really good and I knew she loved me and I loved her more every day. I tryed writing some more short stories but for some reason I couldn't write. After I got all those rejection slips from the publishers, I was beginning to think I couldn't write. Then someone would say that it took years to be a writer and I believed it or like my dad always said "Sharon your nuts, I never even knew no writer that ever amounted to anything. You have to get a good job to amount to anything." Well I was a good old dish washer and my dream of college I knew now was really a dream.

Each night when we went to bed, it was a first time all over again. I loved her soft shoulders uncovered as she lay next to me and the moon sat on our window sill and then she would come to me. Our bodies touching and our lips meeting. She loved my hands and I could feel the shivering of her body at my touch and her wispers of love. I just shook all over and some times I felt like I was going to die because I was so full. We would make love for hours and some times until day break. Always together and filling each other with all the love we had. I can remember laying there with her in my arms and thinking I was so greatful, I was so lucky and I was happy for the first time in my life.

Chapter Nineteen

I never realized how
hard it was to go gro-
cery shopping. Every-
thing cost so much and
we only had a certain
amount to spend on gro-
ceries. At first every
time we went up to check
out I would be scared
because I just knew we
would go over the amount
of money we had. There
was always a big line of people waiting and if
you made a mistake everyone would look at you
or get mad because you held up the line. I was
sure glad Bo knew all about grocery shopping.
Bo and I started playing this game, we would
see who could guess the closest to the amount
we had to pay. She was really good at it and
I lost every time. It seemed unbelieveable the
money they charged for the dumbest things. It
was unbelieveable the amount of money it cost
to feed four people. The thing I use to think
the most was "Thank God for hamburger." If
there was no such thing as hamburger we would
have to become vegetarians. There's nothing
wrong with being a vegetarian, my mom said
that was what she would like to be but if it
wasn't by choice and you were use to meat,
that's another thing. On the days Dee went with
us grocery shopping everyone wished someone
would invent some other way to stay alive, besides needing groceries. Would you believe it
took Dee at least three to four hours to buy
her groceries. Bo or I would try and help her
but she had to pick up every can and look at
every label and check and recheck everything.
It was really funny and maddening watching her
shop. Then there was the kids in the car. I
would tell them stories and play games and

yell at them, it was an art being able to sit
in a car with three kids while Dee shopped.
Sometimes we were lucky and got a baby sitter
but that wasn't very often. Wow, I sure didn't
know how my mom and dad raised five kids and
I was beginning to understand them more and
more but I really believed it was easier being
an adult than being a kid and I was glad I
was grown up.

I was learning to be a plummer and a elec-
trician. The pipes were falling apart in the
house, so I put in some new pipe and had to
figure out how to patch up some of the pipe we
could not replace. Have you ever heard of oakie
fixing? Well, that is fixing things with wire
or what ever you have. Also when the sink got
plugged up Banks knew a neat way of unplugging
it. We got a garden hose and shoved it in the
sink and turned it on. There was a wee bit of
a flood in the kitchen but the sink got un-
plugged. There wasn't any outlets in our bedroom for a light. So I drilled a hole through
the wall and run a extension cord in, so we
could have a light. I was beginning to think
I was pretty smart, that was until me and
Banks put up a clothes line that fell down the
first time it rained. Our post holes had cement about a foot around them but when it
rained, cement and all just fell over. We worked for days fixing that clothes line too,
guess we weren't so smart after all.

We had just finished dinner one night when
I got a phone call. Guess who it was, Troy the
guy I went with in the army. He said he had
come to California to marry me. I explained
everything to him and he still wanted to come
up to the house to talk to me. I ask Bo and
she said o.k. Bo was mad at me and she just
kept giving me this dirty look all the time
Troy was there. I told him I was already married and I loved Bo. He sat there for about
three hours trying to talk me into marrying
156

him. Bo was really getting mad. Finally Troy
left still saying some day I would marry him
and I was beginning to wonder if he bumped
his head or something. Troy had gone by my
mom and dads house and my mother got on this
kick for the next four or five months of saying, "Sharon, you should marry that nice looking guy. He would really treet you good and he
really loves you."

Alice, my mom's neighbor across the street
was Bo's best friend until Bo decided to get
a divorce. Alice was even going to try and
stop her from getting a divorce. Alice, had
known me ever sence I was three years old. She
use to live next door to my mom and dad at the
mines and her son was the same age as me. Terry, Alice's son came back from the service.
He was married and had two kids and he and his
wife had a fight and were in the process of
getting a divorce. Terry came over to see Bo,
he and Bo were good friends. It was really
funny because when we were kids Terry and I
hated each other. We had been in love with the
same girl and use to get in fist fights and I
usually won and his mother would tell my mom
on me for beating him up and my dad would say
"That dam kid of yours needs to be beat up."
Usually I got in trouble from my mom when I
got in fights but when ever I beat up Terry I
never got in trouble and Shirley's mom use to
pat me on the back. Grown ups never did like
Terry and I didn't know why.

Terry started talking about Shirley and I
started remembering something I had tried for
years to forget. Terry kept saying that he had
never forgotten Shirley and even tho he was
married he never could forget Shirley. I started hating him all over again for making me remember. I was eight and all of a sudden my
life was beautiful. Shirley and I were together all the time and we had a secret valley. We
walked among the bluebells and poppies holding

hands and she was always smiling and I loved
her so much. She was the most beautiful girl
I had ever seen, with her long curly hair. I
could remember the way she talked and the certain way she would look at me. Terry was always trying to kiss her and following us a-
round. Terry and I were always fighting, except when we use to sing this song to Shirley,
    "Baby face, you got the cutest little baby
face, no one could ever take your place baby
face."
    One day my mom and sister and I went over
to Shirleys house and she was gone. I could
still see that house empty and remember looking in every room but she was gone. I wanted
to scream or hit something, why did she leave
me, my mother said,
    "They left because they didn't like us, so
shut up and forget it."
    I was glad when Terry left and I didn't
like what he made me remember.
    I started trying to play ball again but it
was really hard because I had to work on most
of the week ends and I was really tired when
I got off work. I also was really scared of
the people in the stands and all of a sudden
my arm wouldn't work right. I was so scared I
couldn't throw the ball. I decided to quit and
everyone was mad at me for a while. After the
ball games a bunch of kids would come over to
our house. We started having a lot of parties.
A lot of new kids were coming to the parties
and I would ask if they knew what was going on
and if they were gay and someone would say yes
and for me to quit being so serious about everything. Then all of a sudden everybody was
saying me and Jan made a bunch of kids gay.
Wow, I had so many things said about me, I was
just getting tired of it, that's all.
    One night I caught Jan kissing Bo and I
fliped. I started yelling at them and was really
mad. They both said I was nuts and they weren't
158

doing anything. The next day Bo told me Jan had
kissed her and I ask her why she stuck up for
Jan the night before and she said she didn't
know. I was really jealous of Jan and when I
saw Bo and her together, I thought I was going
to die. I thought that Jan could take anything
away from me. She took Carol away from me and
I thought now she was trying to take Bo away
from me. Then I thought about what Jan had said,
    "Someone can't lose something they don't
have."
    I hated that saying and I thought Jan was
mean and Bo did love me.
    I got a raise at work and so we got a pretty
nice used car and found a small house in Concord to rent. It was the cutest house I ever
saw, it looked like a ginger bread house and
it had a nice big yard and a good school close
by where Rickie could go to school and Nickie
was going to start school also. We were really
happy and all our friends helped us move and
we had a big party. Nom was a artist and was
going to a Art school in Oakland and she brought
us some paintings for our house and she also
built a go cart and painted Rickie and Nickies
name on it. They were really thrilled. The
girls that came to the house always brought
Rick and Nick something and they were getting
spoiled.
    There was a cute little old lady that lived
in the house behind us and even though Jan
offered her a can of beer one night when we
were having a party, she became our grandma.
She was all alone and her family didn't come
to see her very often. She was very lonesome
and so we adopted her. She would come over with
something she baked and watch shin-dig with us.
She was really hip and she was our grandma.
She had lived a awful life. She lived in a
tent most of her life traveling from farm to
farm picking cotton or what ever there was.
Her husband was a drinker and he drank up most

of the money they made and left her and her
little kids in the tent most of the time without enough to eat. I almost cried when she told
me about how her daughter wanted to go to this
dance and how she slipped in and took some money from her husband when he was asleep so her
daughter could get the dress, for the dance.
She also told me about how her husband use to
pull her teeth out with a pair of pliers. She
told about how she got a divorce and how everyone thought she was so awful and her husband
had put in for the divorce and got it on the
grounds that she was mentally cruel to him. She
said she considered herself as a widow lady and
woman and she was bent over with age or from
hard work and she had part of her nose missing
from a cancer that had been removed and she
was very self concious about it. She was a gentel good woman and the sweetest, cutest lady
I ever knew.

Dee was going to rent the house next door
but she had to wait for the people to move, so
she and Banks and Denice were staying with us.
It was about time for Dee's baby to be born
and everyone was real calm about it but it made
me nervous. I had a real bad day at work and
I came home and Bo, Banks and Dee had been out
drinking that day and didn't even have a beer
for me. I was really mad. Sue, one of the girls
on the ball team, came in and said her car had
a flat and she didn't have a jack. Banks said,
   "Come on Sharon let's help her."
   "I don't feel like it."
He winked at me and come over and said we'll
go have a beer. I thought why not Bo's been
drinking all day and didn't even buy me a can
of beer and I'm mad so I said o.k. We went down
to this bar in Concord and sat there drinking
and Banks was trying to put the make on Sue.
Wow, he was to much. Sue started dancing with
some guy and Banks kept saying he was going to
go to bed with her. She came over and sat down

and we started talking about college and I was
telling her how I liked to write. All of a sudden Bo was standing there and she was really
mad and Dee was with her. I tryed to keep on
talking because I wasn't doing nothing. So I
said, "I would like to take a course in Psychology."

Bo was so mad and she kept looking at Sue
and I like we had done something.

"You better take a course in people! Does
your girl friend know how little you know about
people? You better get up right now and come
home or you won't have any happy home!"

Wow, was I in trouble. I got up and started
to walk out, Dee and Bo had went storming out.
Then Banks said,

"Your sure hen pecked! You start letting
them push you around and you'll become a bug.
By god no one's gonna tell me that shit!"

Well, I didn't do nothing. I should be mad
at her she went out today without even bring-
ing me a beer and then her thinking I was trying to mess with Sue. Wow, I'm mad. I sat there
drinking and getting very drunk. Banks said we
better get Sue out of the bar before she went
to bed with this guy she was dancing with. We
left the bar and then Banks stoped and got
some beer and then he drove to this field some
where in Concord. He got out of the car to go
to the bathroom and Sue and I started making
out. Then I started making love to her in the
seat. Then something happened that give me the
worst set of creeps I ever had. I felt a hand
on my hand as I was making love to Sue. I jumped up and turned around and it was Banks. Banks,
had reached in the car and was trying to find
out what I was doing to Sue, he really thought
I was a guy. I got out of the car and I couldn't
get over what Banks had done. Wow, that was
really creepy. I just stood there and everything was so strange. I was really drunk, what
was I doing there and why did I try to make

love to Sue? Banks got in the car and started
trying to make love to Sue and she started
screaming. She yelled for me to help her so I
opened the door and told Banks we better get
back to the house because I knew Bo and Dee
were mad.

The next day Bo took me to work and didn't
speek to me and when she picked me up she said
it was all over between us. She said she knew
that I made love to Sue and we were all through.
I didn't know what to say and I just ask her
please to forgive me and I would never do it
again. She called me everything she could think
of and said she didn't know what she was going
to do. Then she invited Sue over for coffee
and made me sit between them, while they got
in a big argument. I sat there and it felt like
they both hated me and I wished I could just
get up and leave. Then all of a sudden they
were friends and I sure didn't understand what
was going on. Life was getting more confusing
every day and I was beginning to think I was
really dumb and maybe I should take a course
in people.

Well, for three, long, long, long long,
weeks she wouldn't let me touch her and I begin to think she was never going to let me
touch her again and I deserved it. One thing
I thought was, I was really learning about will
power going three weeks without any sex after
you been use to it every night was really something. Banks didn't even get in trouble, he
just talked his way out of the whole thing. He
told me I was really stupid. He said, even if
you get caught right in the act, don't ever
admit to nothing. Banks was really a louse, he
was really rotten to the core. He also said if
he got a chance he would fuck anything. He said
he would stick it in anything and had just about
done it too. Life sure is confusing.

I came home from work and Bo had fixed my
favorite dinner and we watched t.v. with the

162

kids and ate pop corn and I started thinking
maybe she was beginning to forgive me. We got
in bed and I turned over after kissing her on
the head. Wow, I was getting use to just sleeping next to her. Then I felt this warm soft
body rubing on me, at first I thought it must
be my imagination because it had been so long.
Then I knew she was mine again, oh, I needed
her so bad and I never felt anything so strong
in my life as what I felt for her. My hands
were all over her and inside of her and she
hung on to me and moved like she never moved
before and I kissed her and held her and teased
her. She dug her nails in my back and suddenly
it was like an emotional earth quake and we
come together and I thought I was going to
faint and we melted softly in each others arms.
We made love all night long and the thunder
and lightning sounded inside of us and we were
together again.

Chapter Twenty

I usually had to work
on week ends and it
seemed like I always
got the six to two thir-
ty shift. That ment that
on Saterday and Sunday
mornings I had to get
up at five o'clock in
the morning. Usually on
Saterday night we would
have a party or go to a
party and most of the
time I didn't get to bed until three or four in
the morning. I prided myself in being able to
always make it to work. Some of our friends after a week end couldn't even make it to work
on Mondays. I didn't tell anyone but some times
I felt like I was a hundred years old.

I really hated Sundays, I would get off work
at two thirty and be so tired from only getting
about four or five hours sleep in two days and
at home Mike and his relations and his girl
friend would be there. Bo and Mikes girl friend
would be sitting talking about Mike and his mother and brothers and a bunch of other people
would be there. I felt like a stranger in my
own house. One week end Mike and his family were
having a family reunion and he came and got the
kids. I didn't trust him with Rickie because
he was always hurting Rickies feelings or making Rickie feel left out. Bo got mad at me when
I said she shouldn't have let Rickie go. I was
in the back yard when the kids got home and
Rickie came out crying and said he had to talk
to me. He said his dad had introduced him at
the reunion as his step son. Rickie ask me if
that ment that his mother wasn't his mother?
I told him he knew his mother was his mother
and I went in the house and told Bo what Rickie had told me. I could have killed Mike and

164

I don't think I had ever been that mad in my
life. Bo took Rickie in the bedroom to explain
things to him and Mike walked pass me and went
in there and as he passed me he said,
"This is private family business!"
It was a good thing I had self control because I almost hit him. He acted like he owned
that house and everyone in it. Bo came out and
told me she smoothed everything over and if I
agreed with what she told him. She said Rickie
was o.k. I was sure glad of that because he
was really upset, thanks to Mike, wow he made
me mad.

Mr. Smith steped on a nail and didn't pay
any attention to it, he had sugar diabetes and
didn't have good circulation in his legs so he
really couldn't feel how bad his foot got. In
a few weeks he ended up with gangrene and we
found out to late.

The doctors wanted to amputate his foot but
Mr. Smith wouldn't let them. He said his uncle
had sugar diabetes and the doctors started cutting on him and he ended up with his whole leg
cut off and he still died. The doctors took
off his big toe and part of the bottom of his
foot. He had them give him a spinal and he
watched the whole operation. He said he was
going to watch them and make sure they didn't
try and take off his whole foot. Mr. Smith got
out of the hospital but he couldn't walk and
had to use a wheel chair. Paul and him had to
come to live with us because the county wouldn't
give him any money, they said his check had to
be used to pay for his doctor and hospital
bills. Paul had quit school and was trying to
find a job but it was really hard and he was
only sixteen. Paul had a new girl friend she
was twenty one. He had gotten his last girl
friend pregnant and her mother took her to a
doctor in Martinez and got her some kind of
shot. His new girl friend was wanting to get
married and Bo and Dee and Mr. Smith thought

it might straighten him out but I thought he
was pretty young to get married. Paul stayed
in the back bedroom of the house and he had a
different girl in there every night and I
thought that didn't seem like he wanted to get
married. Everyone thought that if he would
just get married that would solve everything
and I was out voted and so I didn't say anything.

I started working over time at the hospital
and looking for a better job. I went to this
electronics company in Concord and put in my
application. The boss said all the women there
had to wear dresses and that he had the sharp-
est assembly line out of all the electronics
companies. They give me a test and said I was
hired. I went through my closet and got out
my cloths I wore in high school and Bo and I
ironed them and fixed them up, so I could start
work in the electronics company. I quit my job
at the hospital and I was really happy getting
away from seeing all those old people suffer-
ing and not being taken care of. It was nice
getting payed every week and I was getting $1.50
a hour. The women at work really dressed up and
they were always going out to lunch and going
places· after work. They would invite me to go
places with them but I had to get home and besides I didn't want to go even if I had the
money and cloths. I also was living in a different world. They couldn't understand how
come a single girl always wanted to stay home
and didn't talk about men and just couldn't
fit in there way of life.

I had worked there about three weeks and I
thought everything was fine. I just did my work
and went home and everyone acted o.k. It was
Friday the fourth of July and Mike and his girl
friend Jeanie were going to spend the week end
with us and we were going on a picknic and
watch the fire works in Concord. My boss called me in the office and told me that I was a

good worker and everyone liked me but they had
lost a contrack they hired me for and there
wasn't enough work for them to keep me. I said
o.k. and got my check and left. I really didn't
think about not having the right cloths and
not fitting in with there extra curricular activities, I believed my boss and about a year
later I realized what had happened. Some times
I can really be dumb. I didn't tell Bo about
it until the weekend was over because I didn't
want to spoil the weekend.

I started looking for another job on Monday
and by Wendsday I had gotten a job through a
employment agentcy and I owed them another
$245.00. This guy that owned a machine shop
was inventing a remote control system for slot
cars. The job was really interesting and my
boss let me help him think up different idea's
and we started working on all the problems that
go with an invention. My boss also started
teaching me how to run the different machines
in the shop. He had a contract with the government and made the firing mechanisms for there
rifles. We invented the remote control only to
descover that another company had invented a
less costly remote control and so after four
months I had to find another job.

I got a job working as a silk screener for
a printed circuit company and the boss said I
was really good at silk screening and that he
had about a dozen people try out for the job
and they couldn't do it and one guy had silk
screened for about twenty years. He said he
was building a whole new silk screening de-
partment and I would be in charge of it and he
was going to give me a raise. I liked the job
but him and his wife were always having these
awful fights and he was really mean to her. I
just couldn't take that and I would get so upset and shake and be a nervous wreck. Bo really
got mad at me when I quit and she was getting
desgusted with me.

167

Well, I got another job working in the kitchen at another convelescent hospital. I decided I was going to keep this job if it killed me and I was really tired of changing jobs.

My mom called me and she was really upset, she ask me to come over, there was some trouble and she was scared. I got in the car and drove over to my mom and dads. Kerry had left her husband and he had come after her and kicked in mom and dads front door and slapped my dad around. When I got there the police had Bill in the police car and everyone was really upset. My dads eyes looked so funny and I never seen him so beat before.

"I should have knocked the hell out of that son of a bitch."

"Oh hell he's had chairs busted over his head and just kept on fighting."

I swore to myself right then I was going to beat the shit out of Bill for what he did to my dad and sister. Kerry said she was going to devorce Bill and she never wanted to see him again as long as she lived.

Mr. Smith and Paul moved and got there own place. Paul was going to marry Sandy and she had got her uncle the mayor of Martinez to give them a marriage license because they had refused them a license because Paul was only sixteen. Sandy's relation's had aranged for one of the biggest weddings in the county and all the big wigs would be there. I had to work and I was glad.

All the kids were still comming over to the house and Carol and Sue started staying with us. I just couldn't understand Bo, wanting Sue to live there after what happened. She also knew how I use to feel about Carol too. My car broke down and Sue helped me put a whole rear end in it and we changed the brake shoes and rebuilt the carbrater. I got a week off from work and we went to Lake Tahoe. Mr. Smith and Sue went with us and we got a camp ground and

168

then at night we went in to town and gambled.
We really had a wonderful time it was the first
time I was ever there. I was setting at the bar
and it was getting close to two o'clock and I
ordered another drink and was really thinking
I was getting away with something, they didn't
even notice it was two o'clock and I ordered
another drink. Bo and Sue came and sat down
they had been gambling. I laughted when they
ordered a drink and got one and I wispered to
Bo,

"Ha, ha, they don't even know it's two
o'clock."

Bo busted out laughing and told Sue what I
had said and then they both just cracked up.
I ask them what was so funny and then they
told me the place stayed open twenty four hours
a day serving drinks.

I started working over time at the hospital
and got a night job working for this guy that
cleaned movie theaters. I worked days at the
hospital and nights cleaning the theaters. I
never realized how dirty those in door shows
were. My boss said some people that owned
shows never did clean them right and people
could catch something if they went to them. We
started cleaning the theaters after they closed
at night. We used this steam machine for the
seats and floor. Someone had to crawl in front
of the machine and scrape the floor with a
puddy knife and this young girl had to do that
and when she got done working she looked awful
and it was really hard work. Her husband got
to run the steam machine. I scraped gum off
the seats and mopped the floors and stuff like
that.

My mom was really worried about my dad and
said he was really acting funny. I was so busy
and had so many things on my mind I didn't
think much about it. Bo and I went down and
bought some new furniture. We really got a
good deal on it. We got the boys a new bedroom

set. We got a nice living room set and kitchen set and the house really looked nice. I bought Bo new dishes and linnen and a electric mixer. She said she never had such nice stuff before and I bought Rickie and Nickie some new cloths and me and Rickie bought some car models and would sit by the hours working on them. Bo said she always wanted to have one of those real nice model boats. I bought one and built it for her and she said it was the nicest one she ever saw.

I went over to my mom and dads and I couldn't believe what I saw. My dad was sitting on the couch and he was shaking and he kept saying the people next door were going to kill him and kept talking about bugs and my poor mom kept saying she didn't know what she was going to do. My dad couldn't work or anything and he was losing weight and so mom and my brother Bob took him to the doctor and the doctor gave him some tranquilizers but he wouldn't take them because he thought they were poison. I didn't know what to say or to do and so at work I ask one of the nurse's about my dad and explained how he acted. She said we should comit him to a convelescent hospital and he sounded pretty hopeless. I didn't believe her and I thought she was wrong.

I went back over to my mom and dads, I was really worried about my dad and I felt very guilty because I hated my poor dad all my life and now he was so sick and helpless. I was the only person my dad would let cut the hedge around our house. My dad had just bought some new hedge cutters before he got sick. I started cutting the hedge it really looked awful and my mom said my dad was worried about it and so I thought maybe if I could get my dad to help me cut the hedge it would make him feel better.

"Hey dad, would you come and see if I'm cutting the hedge o.k. no one can cut it as good as you can."

"There's to many bugs out there."

"There aren't any bugs dad, come on."

He came out and said it looked o.k. but
then he started cutting the hedge and I stood
there with him until it was cut and he seemed
to feel better. Mom even said he acted like he
felt better. So I went home but I couldn't forget about my poor dad. I really felt bad and
Bo told me my dad would probably be better and
not to worry.

My mom called and said her and Bob took my
dad to the hospital and that he just fell a-
part after he cut that hedge. She ask me to
come and go to the hospital with her. They had
a hearing and me and my mom sat in this room
with all these people and they ask us if we
thought my dad needed help. We both said yes
and my dad was going to be commited to the Napa
state hospital. My mom and dad and I sat and
waited for them to come to get my dad. He was
crying and holding on to mom. He looked so
thin and broken and my mom looked a thousand
years old. A man in a white coat said it was
time for my dad to go. My dad really started
crying and saying we were trying to get rid
of him and he would never see any of us again.
I'll never forget the lost look in his tear
filled eyes and the way he kept looking at us
through the police car window. Then he was
gone, my mom was crying and she said it was
my fault because I shouldn't have got him to
cut that hedge.

Everyone said I should stay with my mother
because she was alone and I was single and
didn't have any responsibilities except to my
mom and dad and the rest of the kids were married. I told Bo I thought I ought to go and
stay with my mom for a while.

"We're your family too and we need you,
Sharon you can't have two families your going
to have to pick one or the other."

I called my mother every night after I got

off work and I went over to visit her every
chance I got but everyone said I was really a
louse for not staying with my mom. I really
started drinking a lot, when I wasn't working
I was drinking and I kept thinking about how
much I hated my dad and how now he was in a
mental hospital and I had helped comit him. It
seemed like a long time ago when he use to beat
me and would get me in a head lock and choke
me until I thought I was going to pass out. I
would try and run from him but he would catch
me and it would be twice as bad. He was alergic
to dust and use to have these scars on his
arms and his arms were always bleeding and he
would catch me and rub my face in the blood.
When I was little he use to lock me in the bedroom without any light on. We use to drive to
town and he would try and run over the dogs
in the streets and when he would run over a
dog he had a hammer in the back seat and he
would get out of the car and hit the dog over
the head with the hammer until it was dead if
it wasn't already dead. I use to think about
killing him, I hated his guts and wanted to
kill him. I thought about all that and then
I thought about the lost eyes of the poor man
that left in the police car. I did love my
dad, I felt so mixed up and I wish I never
hated my dad and what if it was my fault that
he went to that mental hospital. I couldn't
talk to no one and I hurt so bad inside, I
just started getting really drunk and Bo was
mad at me most of the time and everyone was
wondering what was wrong with me.

Chapter Twenty One

The doctors said that my
dad needed shock treat-
ments and they began to
give them to him. My mo-
ther was really worried.
She said, there was a
man in the ward with my
father, that had been
getting shock treatments
for twenty years and he
was nothing but a veg-
table. Shock treatments
didn't work on everyone and the doctors seemed
to think that shock treatments were my dads
only hope.

Mom kept talking about the months she spent
with dad as he slowly sliped into his frighten
world.

"No one can ever know what it was like sitting with your father as he slowly lost his
mind. At times I didn't know if I was sane. At
the end he was such a gentel scared person. He
kept saying, he should be put in a violent ward
but there was nothing violent about him. He
would just sit and shake and worry. He was always worried about bugs and he took a dozen
showers a day. He got so thin and his blood
pressure was so low. If he hadn't gone to the
hospital, he might of died."

I drove my mother to the hospital to see my
father. The long drive was mixed with feelings
of confused morning and regrets that blocked
out the one thin hope that seemed so small and
far away. I felt the strenth being drained out
of my mother and I tried to reach out and help
her but she seemed to be fighting a lonely bat-
tle that only she knew and had to fight. My
parents were both going through a part of there
lives that no one could really understand, a
part of life that was leaving its heavey mark

and made you realize how helpless a human being could be. What is this world all about? Why must there be pain and sorrow? What is it that causes the final event that puts a human mind in the hands of other humans? I don't think they truely know or maybe never can find the answers, to the world of the lost.

A man unlocked a heavy steel door and let us in the ward, my father was staying in. The walls were painted a drab colar and a feeling of sad lonely emptyness was in the musty air. The man took us to dads room. There was a army cot and a small night stand in the corner of the room.

"Mr. Isabell is a very neat guy and very clean, he's always worried about everything being just so. He isn't here so he must be setting outside in the yard. This ward has its own yard."

We walked through the ward on the way to the yard. I looked at the lost faces of the men in the ward and then I saw someone I knew. I couldn't believe it, one of my junior high school teachers was there. I just couldn't believe it, he always seemed so sure of everything and was one of the best teachers in school. I had to say something to him and when I looked in his eyes they were sad but it seemed like he knew me. He was just like he was in school and I couldn't tell there was anything a matter with him. He ask me not to tell anyone that he was there and I promised. I'll never forget this young kid about nineteen that was in there. He just sat and stared at his hands and his hands were limp and revolving from his wrists in weird motions. He was all locked inside of himself and just sat and stared at his confused hands, it was one of the lonliest lost things I had ever seen. When I was about six or seven this family moved to the mines and they had a girl about the same age as I was. There was something mentally

174

wrong with her and they turned her lose in the
hills. She had a dog and her and her dog just
ran lose in the hills. She barked like a dog
and sometimes she would stand on the hill behind our house and bark at me and my sister.
Her eyes were wild and she could run faster
than a deer. Sometimes she would walk on her
hands and feet, I don't think I can ever forget that. The world is so full of hurt people.
What do we do, I couldn't live with myself, I
couldn't pretend that nothing was happening. I
couldn't forget the sights I had seen and I
couldn't forget my dads lost eyes that had
cryed out in the past for help, only to be
closed in because there was no one there to
help him or to see the years of crying out,
that ended up being shocked out of him. Oh, I
didn't want to believe the human race was un-
careing and selfish. All these things were in
my head and my heart felt like it was being
torn out of me. I wished I could do something
because I couldn't forget and I was hateing
myself more and more. I don't understand life
and I can't understand why there can't be at
least as much happiness as saddness.

Dad was not very rational and my mom was
really worried that the shock treatments would-
n't help him. We went to talk to the psychiatrist and I begin to lose my faith in psychology. The psychiatrist didn't ask anything
about my dads background or anything about
him personally. It seemed like they didn't
consider my dad a person but just a case to
be experimented on without any understanding
or care about the human being. I couldn't understand how shock treatments alone could
straighten out a confused mind that had taken
years and deep seaded roots to finally bring
to the braking point. This wasn't anything
like I studied in high school, but the world
isn't anything like they teach you either.
They tell you things that end up to be empty

dreams and at first you think it just must be
you and finally you realize it happens to others too. Then the psychiatrist ask me something
I'll never forget.

"Does Mr. Isabell have homosexual tendencies?"

"No! My father doesn't."

"He isn't responding to the shock treatments as yet but we have just begun them. We
have hope for Mr. Isabell, so if I were you
I wouldn't worry."

Soon as we walked out of the doctors office,
mom ask me what a homosexual was. When I told
her she said,

"Oh my god, why would they ask a question
like that about your dad?"

Besides what was happening to dad, mom was
having a hard time. She was alone and didn't
have any income. Dad never would let her work,
so she had no experience at any occupation and
didn't have any idea what to do or where to begin. They had taken out insurance on the car,
so that if my dad had anything happen to him
the insurance would make payments on the car.
The insurance company wouldn't make the payments and were trying to get out of making them.
Mom spent months writing letters and calling
them before they finally did what they were
supose to. The county said they couldn't help
my mom unless she sold their house. Finally my
dad got a disability check but the hospital
took most of it to pay for my dads hospital
bills. My mom was left with hardly enough money to pay the rent. She scraped and pinched
every cent and kept going some how. She said
maybe if dad got o.k. in a few months they
wouldn't have to sell their house. Mom and dad
worked all there lives, payed all there bills
and were good citizens. Now only a few years
away from retirement they might lose everything. It didn't seem fare, nothing seemed
right or fare.

I worked and I got drunk and I wasn't very

pleasant. The only person that could talk to
me was Rickie. I spent a lot of time sitting
in the back yard. Some how I felt better when
I was outside. My dad had given me this pocket
knife before he got sick, I kept it with me
all the time. Rickie use to come out in the
yard and sit and talk with me. He was one of
the nicest kids I ever knew and some how I
felt that Rickie understood how I felt and I
understood him too. Rickie and Nickie were my
kids and I loved them very much.

Bo and I were beccoming strangers, we had
been happy for two years and now we were drift-
ing a part. It seemed like we were pushing and
pulling each other but we couldn't come together. She didn't understand how I felt and I
couldn't explain how I felt. She didn't think
I loved her and she said by the way I acted
no one believed I loved her.

One night we stopped by Janice's house and
I was drunk. I layed on Janice's couch and her
and Bo were sitting on the floor talking. I
started to fall asleep and when I opened my
eyes, I saw Janice touching Bo, she was running her hand up and down Bo's leg. I got up
and said,

"I'm leaving you can stay if you want!"

I walked out the door and got in the car.
Bo came out of the house and got in the car.
Janice came out and reached in the car and
grabed me by the shirt.

"Get out of that car and I'll beat the shit
out of you and your dirty mind."

"Take your hands off me Janice!"

She pulled the car door open and kept yank-
ing on my shirt. Then we were rolling on the
ground and hitting each other and I really hit
her one right in the face. Bo came over and
pulled us a part.

"Sharon you dirty bitch, you get out of here
and don't ever come back."

"Go straight to hell Janice."

177

Janice told everyone I was crazy like my dad and came in her house and gave her a black eye for nothing. I was crazy jealous, everyone knew she would never make a pass at Bo.

Bo said she was going to get a job. I told her to go ahead but jobs weren't that easy to find and it was easyer staying home.

"Like hell it's easyer staying home, you should just try it, it isn't any dam picnic. I'll gladly put in eight hours and get someone else to put up with all the temperamental shit that goes along with being chief cook and bottle washer."

Bo got a job driving a lunch wagon. In a couple of weeks she was making more money than I was. Having more money helped us with the bills. I didn't see Bo much though. Our days off were different and I worked quite a few nights. Then she told me that they needed another driver where she worked, so I put in a application and got the job. I really liked the job. I drove this truck that had been fixed up with coffee urns and a side door that opened and had food in it. We sold soft drinks, gum, candy, sandwitches, cigarettes, cigars, just about everything. We drove around to construction sights. We went around to pipe line crews and factories, building sights, every kind of outside working crews. I liked working outside more than anything and I liked asking questions about the different jobs and learning a lot of new things about construction, that I hadn't been told by my dad. My dad had taken me to work with him when I was younger and he always explained all the different jobs and machines to me. Dad was always going to teach me to run a cat. (bulldozer) He use to tell me when he retired he was going to buy a cat and have me run it and he would be my boss.

Bo liked to talk and she was a very friendly person and she was interested in all the

178

women and things that happened at work. She had
also been around straight women more than I had
and had a lot in common with them. I stuck to
myself most of the time but I liked everyone
and wanted to join in. I just didn't know much
about talking and I didn't want to say anything wrong and have everyone find out about
us. This new girl came to work and everyone
thought she was grate. She had the hearts of
everyone there. She had left her husband and
he had her kids back in Texas and she said she
was going to save all her money to get her kids
and bring them to California. First everyone
was going to take up a collection and then they
decided that some of them would drive her back
to Texas to get her kids. Bo just came up to
me and told me she was going to drive Claudia
to Texas. I got mad and told her she could of
at least ask me about it before she made up
her mind. I thought it was really nice of all
those women to help Claudia like that and I
thought it was a awful thing for a woman to be
separated from her kids but it seemed like all
anyone could think or talk about was Claudia.
She was number one at work and she started
comming home with us every night and then her
and Bo would just sit and talk and act like I
wasn't even there. Bo stayed after work and
went to a couple of parties at some of the womens houses and said she knew I didn't like
stuff like that. Her and Claudia were together
more than she and I were. Claudia was supose
to be saving her money and she was buying new
cloths and got a car and a bunch of stuff. It
looked to me like she wasn't so worried about
getting her kids. I was beginning to think she
was a hustler. I made a mistake and told Bo
what I thought.

"Well Sharon everyone understands Claudia
but you, I use to think you were compassionate."

"I don't care what everyone thinks, there's
something about her, I don't know maybe I'm

179

wrong, I'm just telling you what I think. She's over here all the time too, does she have to come over every night?"

"I don't think your a very good judge of people Sharon and I just wish you would try and be nicer. She is all alone and it's going to be a while before she can get her kids."

My dad came home and everyone said he acted just like he use to. He seemed like he was much nicer to me. Dad and I went to the store to get some beer and he wanted to stop at this bar because he said he wanted to talk to me. We sat there and he began to tell me what he went through in the mental hospital.

"Those shock treatments are just like dying. Everytime you get one it's just like dying and you don't think you'll ever come back. I wouldn't comit a dog to a place like that. I'll never forgive you guys for putting me in there."

Mom kept worrying about dad going back to the hospital but dad got stronger and the doctors said he could go back to work. He had worked at the construction company for fifteen years and when he went back to work they told him they would have to consider him as a new employee and he couldn't go to any of the company meetings. He couldn't go to the Christmas party they were going to have or have any of the privileges he had before he got sick. I wished I could go over and spit in there crummy faces or knock the shit out of them. My dad had worked his guts out for that crummy dam company and he gets sick for less than a year and he is at the bottom of there list. Your expected to lay out your blood and guts and when it comes to rights, you don't have none, oh ya, unless you own a company or have the good fortune and don't ever get sick or have troubles, your on your own to rot.

A week before Christmas my boss called me in the office and told me she was going to lay me off and give Claudia my truck because her route was more important than mine. Claudia came over to the house and said she hoped I wasn't mad at her or thought she tried to get my truck. I told her I didn't think that and the boss said she would hire me back when things picked up.

Mom and dad were going to have Christmas dinner with us and everyone in my family sent us a Christmas card for the first time. Rickie wanted a new bike more than anything and I knew how he felt because I can remember how much I wanted my racing bike before I got it. The year before I had spent hours sanding down

181

Rickies old bike and painting it and putting
high risers and a banana seat on it. This year
he would have his new bike and it was a sting-
ray, like he wanted. It was going to be the
best Christmas we ever had. We had all the
presents that everyone had always wanted and
didn't think they would ever get. Me and Rickie and Nickie decorated the tree and really
had fun. Mr. Smith was the happiest I ever
seen him and just went around smiling.

It was Christmas eve and Bo called me on
the phone and said she had to tell me something. She told me she had slep with Claudia
and that Claudia loved her. I said I didn't
care if she slep with Claudia, just come home
and never see Claudia again.

"Sharon, she loves me!"

"What about me, I love you too."

"I'll come home and we'll talk."

Bo and Claudia walked in the house and it
was all I could do to keep from exploding. I
ask Claudia if she was going to have Christmas dinner with us. She said no and then she
left. Bo wouldn't look at me and wouldn't
talk to me. When we went to bed I started making love to her and she felt just like she
always did and then she pushed me away and
said, "It's not right!"

I stopped and I felt cold all over, wasn't
right, two and a half years of love making
wasn't right, what does she mean. She turned
her back to me and I layed there, I never felt
so alone in my life, she couldn't mean it, she
couldn't love someone else. This couldn't be
happening, it just couldn't, I loved her more
than anything. How could she just push me away
like that, she always told me how she loved me
to make love to her and no one could make love
like I could. She said she loved me, she pushed
me away, she pushed me away.

Chapter Twenty Two

I was twenty four and I
felt like I was a hun-
dred and twenty four, I
couldn't stop thinking
about the day and night
before, when Bo had told
me about Claudia. It was
Christmas day, a day that
was supose to be very
special, it was and I'll
never forget the date,
December 25, 1966. Rick-
ie and Nickie opened there presents and there
eyes were so full of love and joy. They had
gotten everything they had been wanting and
dreaming about for so long. For once they were
over to the neighbor kids house first, to show
them all there presents. We didn't have to explain how it was the thought that counted and
the love, not the gift. We didn't have to say
maybe next year. I never heard Rickie or Nickie say anything to the neighbor kids about
having better presents, I think they remembered how that could hurt.

Bo and I sat by the Christmas tree but she
didn't look at me with love in her eyes, she
didn't call me honey or do any of the things
that had ment so much. I felt like I was dead
inside. When our song came on the radio, she
walked out of the room. I could remember the
look in her eyes when I told her two and a
half years before, "This is the way I feel a-
bout you."

"More than the greatest love the world has
known, this is the love I give to you alone.
More than the simple words I try to say, I
only live to love you more each day. More than
you'll ever know my arms long to hold you so,
my life will be in your keeping, waking, sleeping, laughing, weeping. Longer than always is
183

a long, long, time but far beyond forever you'll
be mine. I know I never lived before and my
heart is very sure, no one else could love you
more."

Someone knocked on the door and before long
the house was full of laughing, smiling people.
My mom and dad were really happy and enjoying
everything. Mr. Smith looked like he was going
to bust from all the joy he felt. Paul and Sandy, Dee and Banks and all our friends were in
and out of the house. Everything seemed so wonderful, except when our eyes met and Bo looked
at me with emptyness. We sat down for dinner
and before dinner was over, Bo got up and said
she had to go somewhere. I followed her to the
car and pleaded with her not to leave.

"I love you Bo."

"You don't know what love is."

I watched her and Rickie and Nickie drive
away. I knew it was the ending and I wanted to
die. I went back into the house full of people
and I couldn't talk, finally everyone left and
I sat by the Christmas tree and got drunk. Dee
told me Bo had said to tell me as long as I
was at the house, she wasn't comming back.

I left and when I came back to get my cloths
a couple of days later, Claudia was moved in.
Bo told me our relationship was like the song
"The days of wine and roses."

"Just a passing breese, filled with memories
of the golden smile that introduced me to, the
days of wine and roses and you."

Dee said, "Now you know how Mike felt."

Dee was wrong, Bo didn't do to Mike what
she did to me. Dee acted like she hated me, I
sure couldn't understand what was happening or
why.

I can't remember how many weeks I woke up
and went to sleep with a can of beer or bottle
of wine. I can remember looking at the clock
at every hour of the day and thinking what we
use to do at that time. Every woman looked like

Bo and every kid looked like Rickie or Nickie.
Every t.v. program was about families, every
song I heard was a sad love song. The cold
emty bed, oh how cold and emty. In the two
and a half years I had only slep away from Bo
one night. I didn't know what to do or where
to go. I didn't know how to fill the lonely
days and nights. I couldn't think or feel, I
couldn't kill myself because I was dead.

"Green fields are gone now parched by the
sun, gone are the valleys where rivers use to
run. I'll never know what made you run away,
but how can I keep hoping when dark clouds
hide the day. I only know theres nothing here
for me, nothing in this wide world left for
me to see."

Green fields, the shadow of your smile,
you've lost that loving feeling, soul and
inspiration and the song I listened to the
most, what now my love.

"What now my love, now that you left me.
How can I live through another day. Watching
my dreams turn into ashes and my hopes into
bits of clay. Once I could see, once I could
feel, now I am numb, I become unreal. I walk
the night without a goal, stripped of my
heart and stripped of my soul. What now my
love, now that its over I feel the world clos-
ing in on me. Here comes the stares tumbling
around me, theres a sky where the sea should
be. What now my love, now that your gone I'd
be a fool to go on and on, no one would care
or no one would cry if I should live or I
should die. What now my love, now there is
nothing, only my last good by."

The bill collectors were after me and my
credit was ruined. Most of my friends thought
it was awful, the way I was drinking and most
of them thought, that I had been the cause of
Bo and I breaking up. Carol and Marty seemed
to be the only ones that understood and they
came over to see me and started getting me to

go places. Mr. Smith said he thought Bo was
wrong, even if she was his daughter. My mother
hated Bo and would sit by the hour and tell me
all these things about Bo. I would get up and
walk out or tell her to just quit talking a-
bout Bo. She would get mad and say I must be
nuts sticking up for Bo after what she did to
me.

I was getting an unemployment check and was
trying to get a job because of all my bills,
but I wasn't having much luck. I had told Bo,
Dee, and Claudia I was going to try and get
my job back driving truck and they had laughed
at me, I'll never forget the way they just sat
and laughed at me, I was truely dead inside,
they killed my feelings. Carol and I would go
to gay bars and straight bars, most of the
time I didn't know or care what was going on.
I would just sit and drink one beer after another until my head was so numb and my brain
wouldn't think.

Its really strange how your whole life can
be broken up in little peaces and you are dead
inside and don't know how you can just make
it through the day. People are around you and
they talk about bread being 31¢ a loaf or if
they should take a vacation or not. I spent so
much time worrying about and trying to please
people. No matter how hard you try you can't
please everyone and by trying all you do is
end up hurting your self. Janice use to say,
"I think of myself first and then I think of
someone else." My mom said, "People care about
people about as much as a chicken does." Maybe they were right, oh well, have another beer
and don't think about it.

Carol and I went to this straight bar during the week. I decided to go to bed with this
guy. He rented a motel room and we went to
bed. I wasn't a virgin any more but I knew I
wasn't straight either. Everyone found out
about it, big bad butch Sharon was going to be
186

a mommy. Then after everyone found out I was
pregnant, I found out that I really wasn't after the second test. That straight bar was really something, the bar tender was running a call
girl service. The only reason I found out was,
I use to be sitting getting drunk instead of
talking and begin to see the things I other
wise might not of seen. The bar tender would
make a call and pretty soon this woman would
come in and he would show her where the guy
was sitting and introduce them. They would
have a drink and then they would leave. The
bar tender was the girl crazyest guy I ever
seen. He was always going to bed with someone.
What I really couldn't understand was, he was
married to one of my high school teachers and
she was the woman of the year. She wouldn't
even say dam if her life depended on it. I
just couldn't imagin them being married.

Rosalee a friend of Dees started running
around with Carol and I. She was straight but
liked to go out and have a good time. Rosalee
was a very sad person inside. She had been
married twice and her last husband beat her
up a lot and she was trying to forget that and
a lot of other things and she was very confused.
She was always laughing and she was very sexy
and all the guys really dug her. Carol and Rosalee would flert with the guys and I would get
drunk. This one night we were sitting in the
bar and Bill my sister Kerrys x husband came
in the bar. My sister was remarried and ex-
pecting a baby. Bill said hello to me and I
said,

"Go to hell."
"Would you like to step outside?"
"Ya."
We went outside and the fight began, I
started sluging him as hard as I could. He
was like a brick wall as we sluged it out.
Some guy came over and broke the fight up. He
was some kind of cop and he said he should put

me in jail because I started the fight.

"That bastard pushed my dad and my sister around!"

He told me to get in my car and leave so I did. The next night when Carol and I went back to the bar everyone in the place bought me drinks for smashing Bills nose.

"Your really a good fighter and that Bills a big bully and he's always pushing someone around."

Some guys I met in that bar were really nice and Carol and I use to talk to them. Then there was the kind that called you a pussy eater or some other dirty name and ask you a bunch of dirty questions. It was beginning to seem like if you were gay, all people could think of was the sex act they emagined in there mind and nothing else, you weren't a human being. You didn't have the right to live in your bedroom the way you wanted. When some of those people ask me those dirty questions, I felt like saying,

"And how many times a week do you screw your partner and in what position?"

This one guy ask me something I'll never forget. He wanted me to tell him how I made love to a woman. We talked for about two hours and I explained every detail from start to finish. I was smashed or I don't think I would of done that or maybe I would have. I was very unpredictable even to my self. He thanked me and said he was going to try what we talked about. Just one more thing.

"I forgot the most important thing."

"Whats that?"

"The most important thing is Love, without that nothing else really matters."

Then I begin to think, who in the hell was I, to be giving advice? In my mind I couldn't really figure out what love was. How could Bo love me and leave me like she did? I knew one thing I couldn't enjoy sex with anyone else.

188

Every woman I went to bed with was a stranger and all I could think of was Bo. I kept thinking of the nights we had spent together and my body, mind, and soul ached for her. I wrote this poem, I called it "What is Love?"

Is love just a physical thing? The touching of two hungry lips, longing and searching. The meeting of two bodies in compleat bliss. Or is love understanding and a joy of just being together with feelings of sincerity and belonging.

What is the real basics of this inexplicable feeling, that can live within a human? A feeling that can drive a persons heart to destruction or to happiness beyond compare. A feeling that can lead a life and hold it helpless in the morning and night.

Think and you will find no answers.

Carol and I went over to Rosalees house. The house was full of people and they were smoking pot. Everyone acted and looked like they were in slow motion. They ask us if we wanted a joint. We said o.k. and started smoking and all of a sudden I was sitting there and kept falling a sleep. Rosalee said she never saw it affect anyone like that before. When I finally got over being so sleepy I felt like I was ten feet high. This guy took out this stuff and everyone started dipping there fingers in it and licking it. Then this guy got a spoon and went in the bathroom and shot it in his arm, it was heroin. When he came back in the room I'll never forget what he said.

"Heroin isn't habit forming is it? Everybody knows it isn't habit forming."

I felt sick and I wanted to get out of there. I walked out to my car and just sat there, I was so loaded I couldn't hold my head up. This real pretty girl came up to the car and ask me if I wanted her to drive me around until I felt better? I said o.k. but she would have to stop

189

and get some gas. I gave her my wallet and she
payed for the gas and took the rest of my money. I didn't descover that until the next day
tho. She drove out to this feild somewhere and
parked the car. She said she wanted me to make
love to her. I was really loaded but I tried
to make love to her and I couldn't do it and
she really got mad. She drove me back to where
she picked me up and then got out of the car
and walked off. I sat there a long time and
then I drove home. The next morning when I woke
up and remembered what happened I couldn't believe it. Then I found out twenty dollars was
missing and I believed it. Wow, some strange
things sure did happen to me. When I told Carol, she couldn't believe it either.

"Sharon, you got rolled."

This one friend of Rosalees worked as a go,
go dancer in Concord and we started going over
and watching her dance. Carol had this big
crush on her. She was really a nice looking
woman and I didn't blame Carol. She was really
to much too, she would dance over to Carol and
I, right in that straight bar and buy us drinks
and people would look at us. Then we met some
prostitutes that were working out of a bar in
Pittsburg. Ramona was the top prostitute and
she was really pretty. I was still getting
drunk and Carol was having a ball with these
straight women. She said there was this one
girl she really liked and was going to ask out.

We went to the gay bars and everyone in the
place was after Carol. She was just having a
ball. I never seen anything like it. If she
went home with someone I went too and passed
out on there couch. We went to parties and I
would get smashed. I would meet someone but
all I could think of was Bo, I didn't want to
go to bed with anyone because it just made me
feel worse.

I would go over and talk to Dee, some how
that seemed to help. Banks beat up Dee and she
190

bought a gun and told him he better keep away
from her. One night when Dee wasn't home Banks
kicked in her front door and took some of her
things. She couldn't get anything done to him
because he was her common law husband they
said. Then one night Banks came to her door
and started kicking it in and so she yelled at
him to stop or she would shoot him. He kept on
kicking in her door, so she shot him and hit
him twice. She emtyed the whole gun at him. It
was on the front page of the paper and Banks
would carry a bullet with him the rest of his
life. He wasn't seriously injured but they
couldn't remove a bullet in his hip. They took
Dee's gun and she didn't know whether or not
they were going to bring charges against her
and Banks was going to try and take the baby
away from her. It was weeks before everything
got straighten out and the charges were dropped and Banks couldn't get the baby.

Chapter Twenty Three

Kerry was very happy
and excited. It was a
week before her first
baby was due to be born.
She did not care if it
was going to be a girl
or a boy. She had been
just looking forward
to having her own baby.
When she use to baby
sit for the neighbors,
the kids liked her so
much that they would cry when there parents
came home. Kerry loved children and they loved
her. I knew she was going to be a good mother
and that was what she wanted most. Kerrys first
marriage was a deep and sad disappointment for
her. Now she had a new husband and when she
talked about him and her hope for happiness, I
realized what a strong woman she had become.

"Sharon, I sure am lucky I met Bob. He is
really a nice guy and he treets me good. He has
had a hard life and knows what pain and hurt
is and he also knows about kindness. He grew
up in the slums and had to help his mother raise
seven kids. He was in love with this girl and
they got in a car accident and she was killed.
It took him a long time to get over it because
he thought it was his fault. He is really a
wonderful guy and I love him. You know Sharon,
after you've been married your used merchandise
and the guys think that your a easy make. All
they can think of is going to bed and they tell
you they know you must miss it. I am really
lucky I met Bob and I love him."

I'll always remember that little girl in
love that was carried away by a salesman con-
artist. She was a woman about to have a baby
now and yet she would always be that innocent
and sweet little girl with the big blue eyes.

I sure was glad I punched Bill in the nose and she said she was too.

A week later Kerry had a little boy. Hours after his birth he.was rushed to the Crippled Childrens Hospital in San Francisco, for a major operation. He had been born without an opening in his rectum. They would have to operate and make an opening in his side which they called a colostomey. If he lived through this first operation there would have to be at least two more major operations within the next year.

My sisters eyes were on the rode ahead as we drove to San Francisco. She had given birth to a baby only to have it taken from her arms and rushed sixty miles away to a large hospital. She was going to see her baby, that we were told didn't have much of a chance to live. My mother sat silent, with her grey hair looking greyer than usual. I didn't know what to say to Kerry. Words kept running through my brain but I couldn't say them. Maybe the words were a prayer, a poem, I don't know. I just didn't want my sister to lose her baby, that ment so much to her. She had waited and longed for a baby so long.

Little child born from my sister and my loving kin. Please fight for your life, so your mom and dad's love for you will win. Tears will always fall, life is sometimes filled with pain but maybe little baby you won't only walk in the rain. A woman waits for the virdict of fate. let the answer be for her motherly love, it is so very grate. I make this plea from the bottom of my heart, please don't let this mother and child part.

"Sharon, my baby's going to live, I know he is. The most wonderful thing in the world is to have a baby. I saw him when they laid him over my stomach to cut the cord. That was the warmest feeling I ever had. My baby came from inside of me and now he is here for me to hold and love and take care of."

I looked at Kerry and she was filled with all this faith and love and she seemed so strong. I never seen strenth like she had. It seemed as if she had made a decision that the baby was going to live and she wasn't going to let anything in heaven or earth take her baby away from her. It scared me because I kept thinking if she lost the fight maybe she would be lost forever.

When we got to the hospital a nurse took us into the baby's room. Kerry walked over to her baby, he was in a glass baby crib. A little baby with a hole in its side, laid there looking so hurt and so sad. Kerry stood next to the crib with a love in her eyes I couldn't begin to describe. She didn't see the defect, all she could see was her dream come true, she had her baby just like she always wanted.

"Can I hold him? Please let me hold my baby."

I didn't think she'd be able to hold him. He looked so helpless so injured lying there with the hole in his side and his feet were bent and looked broken.

"He has club feet, but they can fix that now. Isn't he beautiful? I have my baby."

Kerry sat in a chair holding her baby and she glowed all over and she kept looking at her baby as tho she couldn't believe her wish had really come true. I never in my life seen anything so sad. My mothers eyes were filled with tears and she started to walk toward Kerry and then she said,

"I have to go outside for a minute, I'll be outside."

Kerry didn't even know mom was gone she just sit there holding her baby. My shy little sister, with her big blue eyes trying to breath life into her son, refusing even the thought of desaster, clinging to her hurt little baby.

A doctor came in and he just stood for a moment looking at the woman and her child. Then he walked over to Kerry and put a reashuring

194

hand on her shoulder. Strenth, compassion and
hope were all in his voice as he spoke.

"Mrs. Barker, your son has under gone major
sergery as you know. The colostomey on his side,
seems to be working. In the operation one lung
colapsed but he is breathing pretty well. His
feet can be operated on in the future."

"Doctor he's going to be o.k!"

"There is one other thing Mrs. Barker."

The doctors voice was hardly auditable, and
graver as he spoke. "Your son has a small hole
in his heart, we're running tests on it now."

"My baby's going to live isn't he?"

"We're doing everything we can and we won't
give up."

My sister looked at the doctor and then at
me and then her eyes returned to her baby. The
doctor spoke once more before he left the room.
"If you have any more questions, I'll be glad
to answer them for you."

"Thank you for helping my baby, I just know
he's going to be o.k."

The doctor left the room and I walked over
to my sisters side, I wanted to give her strenth
but I saw in her more strenth and faith than I
had ever seen in any human being. She sat there
holding and protecting her child and rocking
and talking to him. She wasn't going to let a
million to one odds interrupt her love and joy.
Death is always around the corner.

Kerry rented a room and stayed in San Francisco close to her baby. She went to the hospital every day and sat with her baby she named
Bobby. There wasn't very much hope except the
hope in my sisters heart. She sat with and loved the tiney child that began to cry for life
and fought with his feet in casts and a hole in
his side and heart. There would be problem after problem, operation after operation. Little
Bobby would have to fight with his mom and dad
through five major operations. Kerrys name
should have been hope. She will always be a

hero in my eyes and a great woman.

I got a job working for a janitoral service.
I do get some strange jobs. I was glad I had a
job but the only trick was when someone ask me
what I did what was I going to tell them? I
could not tell them I was a girl janitor, because I don't like being laughed at. Let's see,
if you use big words that helps, but I don't
know all that many big words. I got it, I'll
say I'm a Representative of a Janitoral Service. That really sounds classie and every worker is a representative of where ever they work,
so thats not a lie.

They sure are particular in janitoral ser-
vices. There are ten different ways to mop and
wax floors. You can't be stupid about anything
now-a-days. The mopping and waxing was just
the beginning. I also learned to run a heavy
commercial buffer. That is a real scream at
first, like dancing with a grizzly bear. A guy
had my job and he had taught me the route before he left. I wasn't getting as much money
as he had been getting for doing the same work.
I didn't care tho because I really needed the
job.

I worked alone and my hours were from five
p.m. to four or five a.m. and I worked five
days a week. I was kind of scared sometimes because I was always going in and out of dark
buildings. I had to go down back alleys and de-
serted streets and the later it got the more
frightning it was. It remined me of one of
those movies where the world comes to an end
and there's only one person left alone on the
earth. I really felt like that, sometimes I
would work all night without even talking to
anyone. When your alone like that I think you
can really just appreciate people. It was nice
just being around another human being or just
saying a few words.

This one place I went to was a lumber yard
on the outside of town. To empty the garbage,

I had to walk way out in back through these
stacks of lumber to an old box car. I had to
walk inside of the box car to emty the garbage can. I often thought this would be a beautiful place to get hit over the head. Then I
would think, who would want to do that, after
all how many people want anything from a lumber yard? I thought of any logical excuse to
keep from getting scared.

I had made up my mind not to be scared of
the dark. I did not have much of a choice tho.
That was my job working in the dark. I cleaned
this brain surgeon's office once a week. I always opened the door and then went to all the
rooms and turned on all the lights. There was
the waiting room, then the receptionist desk,
a long hall with three treatment rooms and the
doctor's private office. I walked in and went
from room to room turning on the lights. Well,
it was the last treatment room where it happened. There on the floor in what looked like
a gold fish bowl was not a gold fish but a
brain. I was so scared I couldn't move, wow
was that brain ugly and oh boy was I scared.
I kept thinking about this movie I saw about
this brain that took over this guys mind. Well,
have you ever seen those old time silent movies where those people run so fast, that must
of been the way I looked going threw that office. From then on every time I went to that
office I made sure it was before dark and hoped there wasn't any more brains there. On my
days off I use to go and visit Mr. Smith, and
I was sure glad when Friday came.

I liked to go over and visit Mr. Smith, he
and I were really good friends. He was teaching
me all about photography. He was always talking
about us starting a business some day. He and
I both knew we never could but it was fun pretending and it gave both of us something to
look forward to. Bo would leave Rickie and Nickie with him sometimes on weekends. That was the

only time I could see them and Bo didn't even like that. Mr. Smith, Paul, Sandy, Rickie, Nickie and I would go different places. I missed Bo so much, I was beginning to think I wasn't ever going to get over her. I decided that I wasn't ever going to love anyone again. All love does is hurt you.

Mr. Smith was getting sick a lot and I cleaned his house and sit up nights with him when he had attacks and couldn't breath. He remined me of my grandpa and he was so lonely. The house he lived was across the street from the house his wife died in. He said he would be glad when he died.

"Sharon, you would really be surprised if when I died I left you a million dollars."

On Christmas eve me and Mr. Smith went to a drive in restaurant and got some hamburgers and laughed and tried to be happy and not think of the year before. Mr. Smith said he had one wish that he wanted to come true before he died. He wanted to see his favorite program "gun smoke" in colar. I took him over to my sister Billies, so he could see his program on her colar t.v. Billie gave Mr. Smith a big piece of punkin pie and he was really happy. Billie use to cook things all the time for me to take to Mr. Smith.

Mr. Smith had a heart attack and was taken to the hospital. His heart stopped beating for three minutes before the doctors brought him back to life. He just kept getting worse. I went to see him every day. He told me something that really scared me.

"Sharon, I was dead and when your dead there's nothing. You just fade into darkness. You don't know anything. Maybe I won't get to ride my cloud in the sky."

That really scared me because that made me think that what my mother said was true. "When your dead, your dead. You turn into dust. From dust to dust."

198

Claudia came and told me Mr. Smith was dead. She said if I wanted to they would give me one of Mr. Smiths personal belongings to keep. I felt like screaming at her, I don't need anything to remember Mr. Smith, he was my best friend. I don't care what anyone says, he's with his wife on that cloud in the sky and he's smileing.

The funeral was awful and I cryed through the whole thing. I didn't forget Mr. Smith, I couldn't, he was the only person in my life that ever believed in me.

Every chance I got I took flowers and put on Mr. and Mrs. Smiths unmarked graves. I remembered how Mr. Smith always took flowers to his wifes grave and would be so depressed because sometimes he couldn't find it and he was always saving his money so he could buy a headstone for her grave.

Paul fell apart when his dad died and within five months he was in Napa State Hospital. Paul was nineteen years old. They put him through a series of shock treatments but they didn't seem to help. He was permanently committed, he would be in there for the rest of his life. Sandy was left alone, with two small children.

Chapter Twenty Four

One summer night the
sky turned a dull deep
grey color and I could
only see patches of the
starred sky. I thought
it was especially sad
in the summer for the
sky to be so ugly. The
thing I loved most a-
bout the summer was the
beautiful sky at night.
It was really something
to look at the millions of stars winking at you.
The wind was chillie and I felt cold and I turned away from the dull deep grey sky, it remind-
ed me to much of life.

I felt these lost confused feelings and it
seemed like the whole world felt them too. Everyone around me had problems and struggles.
My mom and dad, Kerry, Billie, Charmaine, Paul,
Sandy, and Mr. Smith had them too. I use to go
to this bar and sit. It was dimly light and the
people that went in there seemed to be singing
this sad song together. It was a straight bar
but I felt at home there. This one night everyone got to talking about there jobs and at that
moment I found out another thing we all had in
common.

"I work in a garage and people call me a
greace monkey!"

"I'm a bar maid and people think I'm a slut."

"I'm a truck driver and people think I'm
crude."

"I work in construction and people think I'm
tuff."

"I'm a navy wife and people think I run a-
round with other men."

"I'm on welfare and people think I'm lazy."

My mom told me that everyone has something
that someone can say something about. She said

200

she had a mole on her face that everyone laughed about. She said she got the mole cut off
her face but she never forgot about those people laughing at her but she lived with it. She
said I shouldn't let people bother me so much.

Carol, Rosalee and I started running around
together morc often. We were friends, all three
of us looking for something and none of us knowing what we were looking for. Carol worked in
a bank. Rosalee was on welfare. I was working
for a janitoral service. I guess we were a
strange combination, or maybe someone just wanted us to think that.

Carol was gay but she was very confused and
was getting a lot of pressure from her mom and
from the women she worked with. She was a gay
woman living in a straight world, and that a-
lone is confusing. She decided to start dating
some guys so her mother and the women at work
wouldn't suspect her of being gay. She would
date guys during the week and on week ends Carol, Rosalee, and I would go to the gay bars or
to parties.

Rosalee is a very hard person to describe.
She had three children and had been married
twice. She was a by-sexual but again she wasn't
anything. She told Carol and I more than once,
"I don't know what I am and I don't know who
I am. I wish I knew who and what I am."

Rosalee was always looking and trying to
find herself but she was so confused. She
laughed and she cryed with everyone. People
liked to be around her, she excited people,
and yet no one could get close to her. She had
a sad lonely desperation about her and she
seemed to be crying out for help and yet re-
jecting it at the same time. Carol understood
Rosalee better than anyone and Rosalee would
do anything for Carol and their friendship.

I went over to Carols apartment and Rosalee
was there and Carol was crying and acted like
she was about to have a nervous break down.

Finally she told me what was a matter.

"Sharon, I'm pregnant. I went to bed with this guy I have been going out with. He was beginning to suspect me of being gay. I guess I wanted to try it anyway, to see what it was like."

"Well you might like having a baby. I'll help you take care of it."

"I can't have a baby, I'd lose my job and I will never go on welfare or get married. My mother would just die if she found out about this. I just can't have this baby my whole life would be ruined. I'm going to get an abortion. Rosalee says she will help me. She knows how to give an abortion."

"Carol you can't! It might kill you. I heard some awful things about abortions. I won't let you do it. Please Carol don't do it."

"Sharon, I have to. I can't have this baby, it wouldn't be fare to anyone if I had this baby."

"Rosalee, please don't help her go through with this."

"Carols my best friend and if I don't help her, she'll get someone else."

"She's right Sharon, I'm not going to have this baby, I can't."

I was so scared, I just knew something awful was going to happen. I heard so much about abortions and women dieing. I talked and talked to Carol and I couldn't stop her. I told her about this woman that lived next door to Janice that used a nitting needle on herself and all most died. She said she had more sence than to use a nitting needle on herself and that nothing was going to happen to her. I couldn't stop thinking about it and worrying about what might happen. I loved Carol in a very special way, we had been through a lot together. If anything happened to her it would be my fault because I didn't stop her and yet how could I stop her?

Rosalee gave Carol the abortion and in three days Carol was in the hospital with blood poisoning. She almost died and her mother found out. That is, her mother found out about her having a miscarriage. The doctor ask Carol some questions but no one found out about the abortion. Carol said her mother said she was glad she lost the baby. It would really be the town scandle if anyone found out. Carol said she was glad she did it and if it wasn't for Rosalee her whole life would have been ruined.

Nothing in this world makes any sence. Why do I keep seeing all these things happening around me. I wished I could yell at the top of my lungs stop! Stop! Stop letting me see all these things. My mom told me I was soft and that I had to get some guts. She said you have to be strong in this world because the world is rotten. I fought all my life against believing that. I wanted to believe my mother was wrong but I was beginning to think she was right.

Rosalee worked part time in a bar in Pittsburg. She said she wished she could find a full time job so she and her children could get completely off welfare. I'll never forget the day I took her out to look for a job. She made out applications in about fifteen different places. Some of them said they would call her. We stopped at this bar to get a beer and started talking. We talked about our poems. Rosalee liked to write poems and so did I. I liked writing short stories the best tho. Then she told me about how confused she was and about the psychiatrist she had been seeing. She said she was beginning to think nothing could help her. Then she started opening up to me and I listened and really tryed to understand. Then all of a sudden she said, "You sound just like my psychiatrist, Carols the only one that understands me." Then Rosalee said she wanted me to take her to this bar in Pittsburg. She said,

"Sharon, just promise me one thing no matter what happens don't leave me in there o.k.?"

"O.k. Rosalee."

We went inside the bar and Rosalee really started drinking and acting like she didn't like me. I ask her to let me take her home but she said no. Then she got up and moved to another part of the bar. I kept asking her to let me take her home but she just seemed to get mad at me for asking. I thought promise or not I am leaving so I left her there. I'll never know why Rosalee made me make that promise or if maybe I could have helped her. Carol said Rosalee really liked me but that I talked to much about deep things and she didn't like that. Carol said Rosalee just wanted to be happy but she never was. I guess I'll always remember the way I left her in that bar. I'll always remember the way she through back her head and laughed.

A week later Carol was supose to cut Rosalee's hair but her mom wanted her to take her somewhere. Rosalee went to work down at the bar and she got in a argument with this guy. She went home and her, her little girl and boy were in the front room when the guy came in. He stabbed her while her little boy and girl witnessed it. When her little boy came over and tryed to help his mother the guy cut up the little boys hands. Rosalee died before they got her to the hospital.

"Sharon, Rosalee's dead, she's dead. I was supose to cut her hair. She was murdered, I could have been murdered too. We were so close, she told me things she never told anyone. I can't believe it Sharon, I can't believe it. How could anything like this happen? I just saw her yesterday."

Carol went over and talked to Rosalee's mother and tryed to do all she could to help.

"Sharon do you know what Rosalee's mother told me? When Rosalee was eleven years old

this truck driver raped her and then he got in
an accident and was killed. She went to his
funeral and fell on his grave and beat it with
her fists."

Rosalee's murder was on the front page of
the paper. "City woman slain." Carol walked
around for days confused and tore up inside.
We didn't go to Rosalee's funeral. Neither one
of us thought we could stand it. I watched Carol slowly change and I saw her trying to fight
off the memories that were taking so long in
becomming the past and could never be compleat-
ly forgotten. I begin to hate life and felt all
it was, was a living hell that everyone was being put through.

Carol and I got drunk a lot. One night we
went over to this straight girls house and it
was full of people and they were smoking pot.
Carol and I smoked a joint. I really felt funny. The people were all dancing in slow motion and I had this real relaxed feeling. When
we left I didn't know I was high and started
to walk down these stairs and fell. Wow, I never hurt so bad in my life. I thought I broke
my back. I decided it wasn't very much fun smoking pot. Then we found out it had been soaked
in LSD. That really scared me.

I got another job working in a convelescent
hospital. I just couldn't take working alone
and in the dark, any more. I hated watching
old people dieing too but I had to have a job.
I was beginning to think for some reason I was
ment to see awful things. How could I stand it
if my whole life was going to be like this?

Where is the happiness? Who's got it? It
doesn't have anything to do with being straight
or gay.

I got quite a bit of money on my income
tax return $200.00 I decided to buy a motor
cycle. I bought a yamaha 125. I could ride it
on the freeways and it really ran good. When
I got on that bike it did something to me. It

gave me a freedom I never experienced before. The wind blowing in my face and being free under the stars. Riding threw the mountains and all the colars so true and beautiful. Riding down the freeway sixty miles a hour and looking at all the lights in the night. I was flying and I was free and when I was on that bike I was happy. I begin to feel as long as I had that bike I had hope. No matter how many people laughed at me or no matter what anyone said they couldn't take that away from me. My Freedom!